CROSSINGS 23

# Resistenza Rap

# Resistenza Rap

Music, Struggle, and (Perhaps) Poetry
How Hip-Hop Changed My Life

Francesco "Kento" Carlo

Translation by
Emma Gainsforth
Siân Gibby

BORDIGHERA PRESS

*Library of Congress Control Number:* 2018955742

Printed in the United States.

Published by
BORDIGHERA PRESS
John D. Calandra Italian American Institute
25 West 43rd Street, 17th Floor
New York, NY 10036

CROSSINGS 23
ISBN 978-1-59954-128-0

# TABLE OF CONTENTS

## RESISTENZA RAP

# A Calabrian's Sonic Resistance

Joseph Sciorra

Kento's memoir *Resistance Rap* is a sort of literary road movie, an episodic travelogue mapping the author's journey as an Italian rapper and political activist. Interlocking snapshots trace a miscellany of events—encounters and concerts, recordings and rallies—that collectively recount both the Italian artist's development and his nation's challenges. In the book's opening pages the reader hitches a ride with Kento as he pulls into an anonymous Calabrian town in the Locride region, a bastion of the organized crime syndicate 'Ndrangheta. Kento's band Kalafro is traveling to promote its new album in a minivan clearly marked on its side with the words "Vehicle Confiscated from the Mafia" (*Automezzo Confiscato alla Mafia*) referencing the fact that the car was purchased with money garnered from the sale of mafiosi-owned properties confiscated by the government. The tension is palpable for the passengers until a chance encounter assuages the group's fears: They pull alongside another vehicle whose middle-age driver is blasting the band's music.

Kento (the *nome d'arte* of Francesco Carlo) is a child of Calabria, and through his memories, stories, and rap lyrics, included here in the original Italian and in English translation, he recounts his movement toward his unique pairing of aesthetic sensibilities and social engagement. Written for an Italian audience familiar with the country's hip-hop scene and its anti-Mafia battles, the memoir may create challenges to readers unfamiliar with historical and contemporary features of Italian life. Yet, by detailing one young man's personal, lived experiences it offers the curious reader a unique portal to become acquainted with present-day Italian culture.

Kento takes his artistic cues from those pioneer Italian hip-hop artists who emerged from the *centri sociali*, the abandoned and subsequently occupied buildings that served as community centers and the incubators of the nascent *rap italiano* scene during the 1980s and early 1990s. Those artists—as well as the singer-songwriters (*cantautori*) of the 1970s whom Kento namechecks—addressed such burning social issues as the Mafia, government corruption, neo-fascism, and the exploitation of immigrants, to name but a few. This artistic militancy has long gone out of fashion in the contemporary world of Italian hip hop, so it is all the more intriguing that Kento positions himself as part of this lineage.

As a rapper actively committed to social justice in his art and life, his work participates in what he calls "sonic resistance" to exploitation and injustice—a phrase that is the apt name of one of his albums too. This "son of brigands," as he calls himself in the song "Vengo da Sud" (I Come from the South), is cognizant of Southern Italy's history of *miseria* that resulted in the migration of millions of working-class people throughout the world. For example, in the song "All'orizzonte" (On the Horizon), he declares his personal connection to the Italian diaspora while linking Italian emigration to the pervasive xenophobic and racist politics enacted against current immigrants in Italy:

> Even if I had family all over, not just in northern Italy
> In Switzerland, in Canada, in Argentina, Australia

Blood of my blood, scattered over the map
I still hate that immigrants get looked down on

Historical antecedents of political struggle within Italian transnational activism serve as models for a reclaimed past in Kento's music, perhaps best illustrated in his song "Sacco o Vanzetti" (Sacco or Vanzetti), from the album of the same name, about the immigrant anarchists executed in 1927 after an infamously prejudicial trial:

Vanzetti Bart, only guilty
Of hating the injustice of the system and its rules.
Of being Italian, anarchist, emigrant,
Unionist, antifascist, militant
And my people no longer recall the past

But perhaps the most targeted subject of Kento's "resistance rap" is organized crime and in particular the Calabrian-based 'Ndrangheta. One song in particular is a testament to his commitment and engagement with this ongoing fight: "Denise" is a moving rap about Denise Cosco, a woman born into a 'Ndrangheta family but who bravely broke its code of silence by cooperating with government investigators. After her mother, Lea Garofolo, was viciously murdered for helping anti-Mafia judiciary, Denise took up Lea's mantle and served as a state witness, eventually helping convict her mafiosi father and boyfriend. Rapping about this "young warrior" (*giovane guerriera*), Kento sees this Calabrian woman as an exemplar:

so I repeat: I wouldn't have had her courage
but I try to keep my back straight, like her.
Imagine if you lost everything, like confronting grief
take your dry heart and make it become a fruit.

With this song Kento recognizes the particularly gendered dimensions of an exploitative culture, while importantly offering a formidable female protagonist as a model for liberation and hope.

Throughout the book, Kento pays tribute in small and sundry ways to the African American giants — Biggie, Tupac, Public Enemy, The Roots — who influenced his particular contribution to the international hip-hop nation. But it doesn't stop with music for Kento is also conversant with the works of political activists and writers Angela Davis and Amiri Baraka. He is interested in learning from the black American struggle and applying aspects of that experience to the prevailing conditions in Southern Italy. The name of one of his bands, Kalafro, cleverly plays on the possible affiliations of an Afro Kala(bria). He makes those connections explicit in songs like "Caro fratello" (Dear brother) and "Hazet 36," when he references Rosarno, the Calabrian town where African immigrant farmworkers famously rebelled against living and working conditions of the 'Ndrangheta–controlled orange trade (2010).

It is hard to fully appreciate written rap lyrics in translation, given the loss of rhythm and rhyme of the original language and the abundance of specific local cultural references. For those unfamiliar with Italian who go on to find Kento's music after reading his memoir, he offers in these pages three ways to discover his work: first, obviously, through the music, the beats themselves, followed by the lyrics, the poetics of his art. But Kento suggests a deeper "third level" in which the listener, through his memoir, can understand, as he writes, and "wants to expand the subtext and the references that made me write those words. This is the level that reflects my study and inspiration" (23). Thus, through reading his memoir, future listeners of his music have a guide for familiarizing themselves with the broader context for his "resistance rap."

The odyssey recounted within these pages traverses time and space in order to bear witness to an individual's developing artistry and commitment to political activism. In doing so, Kento chronicles the ongoing dynamics involving the potential of rap music's Italianate permutations and the legacy of a progressive, left cultural politics—what Antonio Gramsci called the national-political—to renounce such societal ills as neo-fascism, xenophobic racism, and misogynistic violence plaguing twenty-first century Italy. Kento's sonic resistance offers a model in which an informed individual's actions and artistry contribute to a larger movement.

# Introduction to the American Edition

Francesco "Kento" Carlo

I had no intention of bringing *Resistenza Rap* to the United States. Not out of distrust for the American reader nor for my text. Not for the bitterness of the historical and political context, which indeed requires that global resistance weaves its experiences into a single body of struggle and thought. Not, of course, for snobbery nor for fear of the language barrier.

But, alas, the cultural barrier is a different matter. It is not enough to convert Celsius into Fahrenheit and to riddle the text with notes. We need to give the reader a key in order to better understand, a key that is honest, engaging, accessible. We need to contextualize. Draw a road that starts from the suburbs of Reggio—made of sun, stories, pride, blood, and scattered dramas—and brings you cross the Atlantic without that blood drying up and those stories being diluted.

Anthony Tamburri and Joseph Sciorra have been formidable allies in this endeavor, together with my Italian publisher Luigi Politano, without whom the book would not have seen the light of day in the first place. They gave *Resistenza Rap* solid roots precisely in the place where rap was born: what is largely a travel story is thus, to conclude, metaphorically, with a Homeric return home. The circle of the story closes in New York City, which gave birth to what is my reference point for my own vocabulary, though obviously filtered by the warm wind of the central Mediterranean. I now land in New York. This time seriously, after visiting it a couple of times as a tourist. Of course, I arrive without the enormous pressure and difficulty of my ancestors who stood in line for registration at Ellis Island, or—at least in a specific case—they hid undocumented immigrants among the coal in the ship's hold. But their stories handed down to us are an indelible subtext to each of my words, so please keep them in mind when you read me herein.

From this perspective, I find particularly intriguing the subtitling "Resistance Rap," which maintains the rhythm but offers a different interpretation. In Italian, in fact, "Resistenza Rap" can be paraphrased as "resistance done through rap," while "Resistance Rap" could be read even as "discourse about resistance." Perhaps a more ambitious approach, certainly in line with the international breadth that—with humility but also with conviction—we are trying to give to this new phase of the project.

I am writing this introduction in June 2018. Today is a beautiful day and—as far as I am aware, it is a terrible Italian stereotype—the plants of sage, mint, and rosemary on my balcony keep me company with their scents and their various shades of green. During these days, in fact, on the other side of the Alps, we have begun to work on the French translation of the pages you are about to read. In some ways it will be a simpler task, given the close linguistic and cultural kinship between the two countries. In this endeavor, I specifically asked that students be involved, and I'm glad to present them to you: they are young people from the Lychee Thierry Maulnier of Nice, led by the Italian teacher Anna Maria Casella.

I'm happy to think that this trip involves them too, as it involves the Italian Hip-Hop veteran Masito, author of the cover artwork that we have decided to keep for this edition, the legendary DJ and producer IceOne who wrote the original introduction, the translators Emma Gainsforth and Siân Gibby and all the many others who, at every level, have helped and supported us, even if only with their encouragement.

And this journey, in the end, involves you as well, American readers or if only English readers, whom I approach with respect and enormous curiosity about the feedback you will give me. I do not come to teach rap in the place where it was invented: I come to tell you how this form of expression has become, also on the other side of the world, the voice of the rebels and the marginalized, and not just for money, hedonism, superficiality. I come to tell you a story that you do not yet know. I hope it changes your life as much as it has changed mine.

# Prologue

We're driving along the 106 Jonica, the notorious *death road*. In some towns of the Locride region it's so narrow it becomes an alternating one-way alley. On August days like these the light here is white-hot, and the air-conditioning in the minivan is on full blast. On one side the name of the band, KALAFRO, is written in capital letters. In smaller letters, though still very visible, it says, VEHICLE CONFISCATED FROM THE MAFIA. We have a concert this evening: We're touring the South to present *Resistenza Sonora*, our concept album dedicated to the fight against the 'Ndrangheta, defined by one journalist as "the first mafia-produced record," because in part it has been financed with the revenues from the properties seized from the Mafia bosses.

We decided to set off a couple of hours before schedule; we know that anything can happen along this road. In fact, entering the town, we are forced to slow down until we stop, and from there we advance at a walking pace. Everyone stares at our brightly colored van, the message on it could not be more explicit. My girlfriend shifts uncomfortably in the backseat. She has just finished *Dimenticati*, a book that tells the terrible story of the almost three hundred innocent victims of the 'Ndrangheta.[1]

The plastic and metal box with smoked glass is the only barrier between us and the forty-plus degrees celsius outside. The air is rarefied, time goes by in slow motion and seems to stop altogether. The scenario is that of a western:

---

[1] The *'Ndrangata* is an organized crime group centered in Calabria (Trans.).

I wouldn't be surprised to see Gian Maria Volonté appear from one of the side streets in the role of Ramón Rojo.

A car driving in the opposite direction pulls up next to us in front of a bar. The street is blocked and we have to wait for it to pull up beside us, but the driver stops, lowers the window, and gestures to us to do the same. Simone, the youngest member of the band, is behind the wheel. He hesitates, then decides to roll down the window. There is complete silence for a fraction of a second. Then the air is filled with music, our music, coming from the car next to ours. The guy, in his fifties, breaks into a smile that to us is wider than the 106 Jonica and adds: "Great job, keep going!"

And we do keep going, we go our way and he goes his until we lose sight of each other in the rear-view mirrors, in a cloud of torrid August dust.

❧

My first memories of roads are from the 1980s: In the neighborhood there isn't even a bar, a pizzeria, a newsstand. As kids, our days are spent on the *timpa*—the dirt road that passes behind the church where we play soccer and the local branch of the Italian Communist Party. The branch is called "Girasole"[2] and as a kid I think it's strange, though I like the idea that it's called after a flower that turns its head to follow the sun, its fresh seeds, with a good rustic taste, that crackle between your teeth. Some years later they explained to me that it was a different flower the comrades wanted to remember: Rocco Girasole, a very young farm worker from the Basilicata region who

---

[2] "Sunflower" (Trans.).

was killed by the police during the farmers' riots in the 1950s: "He was a bit older than you," they tell me, and I try to picture his face.

The party's branch is a few meters from the elementary school and about one meter from the blacksmith's shop—the *forgia*, as we used to call it—so black it could really be a volcanic cave, dotted with blinding flashes of light, grave laments coming from the inside, a strong but not unpleasant smell of hot metal being hammered. In the afternoon, on our way to the party, we stop and gaze at the orange sparks, standing at a distance to avoid being hit, but close enough so it doesn't look like we're afraid. I sometimes think that blacksmiths must be really amused by the fact that to us their shop and what they do are enshrined with an aura of mystery and of extreme danger.

I can still see our old comrade Ciccio Nava opening the heavy padlocks and the reinforced door of the party's offices next door. The special door is one of the two precautions that have been in place since the 1970s, when the fascists exploded a paper bomb here, trying to intimidate the participants of a meeting. The other precaution—it was shown to me only some years later and only after I'd sworn to secrecy, an oath I break only now—consisted of a couple of nailed clubs well hidden near the ice-cream counter, covered in dust, because luckily no one ever had to use them.

The first room is filled with the sweet smell of chewing gum and packaged ice-cream and also retains the magic of the first video games I ever set my eyes on. The second room is generally off limits and is used for meetings and special occasions, the walls are covered with colorful manifestos bearing the symbols of the farmers, the factory workers, and the intellectuals. On the back wall, next to

Lenin's profile, the large and intelligent eyes of Marxist philosopher Antonio Gramsci seem to be smiling at me from a simple pencil portrait. At the age of seven the only thing I know about Gramsci is the tale of the hedgehogs gathering apples.[3] That's enough to make me like him; it reminds me of the bedtime stories my dad tells me.

Growing up I earn the trust of the old militants who tell me about WWII, the persecutions, the struggles. Some tell me they used to own a rifle when they were young. They never turned it in but buried it instead, waiting for the day the Party would summon them to take part in the revolution. Today, as I write about it, many of my old comrades are underground, just like their rifles, and the revolution has not yet come. The Party's offices are no longer there, but the eyes of Gramsci keep staring at me from the wall of my room and seem to be implying something about the "optimism of the will."

"RC Confidential"
(from the album by Kento & the Voodoo Brothers Radici)

*Tonight is calm, and this sand's still warm*
*And the smile that I imagine but still doesn't show*
*Throws out thoughts like a web on the beach*
*It's an old losing game, a fever I caught;*
*It's the bitter honey of strong memory*
*Even bigger in the darkness: RC Confidential.*
*'Cause if it rains, the water all disappears*
*Blood is thick, and leaves its trace on the streets;*
*I think of the shouts in the hood, and of the signs;*

---

[3] This comes from the stories and fables for his children that Gramsci wrote from prison.

Of faith of my friends, of the arrogance of power
Laundry hung out, veiled women in church
And my sketches in the notebooks for the expense accounts
Brigands, Aspromonte, the sea, the island
And as they say at least in theory the threat of the bridge.
The future is today; I don't know anymore
If I should smile, lose heart, or just sing the blues.
Mixing harmonies, false notes, ruckus and quiet
The city's got a thousand secrets, including its own rhythm
When it talks to me, I have to repeat it
And no silence is golden; ask how much it cuts
For the guy in jail, who has sunshine in spurts
The one who dies just to be resurrected,
The one in handcuffs, ask the refugee, the saints, the masks
The gold around the neck, the iron in the pocket, he who goes back
Who sleeps in a ditch and dreams of California
And old refrains live on in new wounds
between the memories in the stories, gunpowder's smell
Censor the article, says, "Nothing consequential"
I rip up the paper, not believing what they say
So, I don't care about your money: it's fake
Or being the best that the market can bring
I'm with the guys in the street, with little at hand:
This place is too big; this place is not enough for me
There's just the writing it, living it, while the words are still murdering
Love and make them ours, maybe more than they say
Keep them warm in our palms and tight like a weapon
Because it is what it is, and sound is life in conversation.

There's just the writing it, living it, while the words are still murdering
Love and make them ours, maybe more than they say
Keep them warm in our palms and tight like a weapon
Because it's what I am, my sound: Reggio Calabria

＊

Rap bursts onto the Italian musical scene during my school years. The story actually starts much earlier, in places like the historic Muretto in Milan or the Teatro Regio in Turin, where the b-boys were already gathering at the beginning of the 1980s, improvising rhymes and spray-painting walls. All this reaches Reggio Calabria in a mediated and muffled way, through the few channels then available. The capital of hip-hop in Calabria at the time is Cosenza, with its social center at Gramna, Radio Ciroma, and above all South Posse and Dj Luigi's Minamò Squad.

Together with Luciano, who sits next to me in class and has been my friend since kindergarten, we basically learn by heart all the cassettes and the fanzines we can get our hands on. A trip to Rome means we can go to the Feltrinelli bookshop in Largo Argentina and buy all the available copies of *Alleanza Latina*, the bible of the young aspiring hip-hoppers at the time. From Milan we receive a videotape with recorded MTV shows: Run DMC, the Beastie Boys, but also Public Enemy and even The Disposable Heroes of Hiphoprisy. Our English is still very basic, but when you listen to Michael Franti sing, it doesn't take much to understand that television has become the drug of the country, or when Chuck D blows up the limousine of a racist politician who wants to cancel Martin Luther King Day.

We start to hang out with the rappers of the area. To us they are surrounded by the mystic aura of superheroes, and we buy our first checked shirts and basketball sneakers. The names of the main bands still bear the taste of those years, and I remember them with the same respect I had at the time: Sfaida Posse, Fuori Fase, Effetti Collaterali.

The first rhymes I write are harsh, disconnected, rigid. I persist, I get kicked in the ass and get encouraged, I step into the first stages with hardly any success, I ask for advice on how to improve. One of the first pieces of advice given to me that is still valid today is: Listen to good music. I write down about twenty lyrics in a large notebook with a hard green cover. I throw them all away. Another twenty follow. Everyone uses a stage name, I choose the name of a character from a cartoon: a prince who drives a modular robot and fights to take back his galactic empire. He finally wins, but he understands that the right thing to do is to proclaim a socialist people's republic (*socialist* and *people's* are not my free interpretation). At the end of the 1990s the first thematic chatrooms appear, in particular *#hiphopitalia* on *Mirc.com*, and to us it seems like the definitive innovation, to be able to chat in real time with other people from around Italy who share our same passion. *YouTube* is so far off, it's a concept we can't even imagine.

At a certain point the rhymes start to come on their own, to talk to one another, to become fabric. I receive my first compliments, I move to Rome, I start to see my name on posters and flyers for concerts. Still today it sometimes strikes me that I make more money in one evening than a factory worker makes in several days. In short, it seems to me that I've fooled the organizers and the audience, who give me money to do something that is good and enjoyable to me more than to anyone else.

*"On the Horizon"*
*(from the album* Sacco or Vanzetti*)*

*Born in Calabria, second half of the '70s*
*In a family that struggled to stay in the black*

*Barely learned to speak just to babble "Hello"*
*We emigrate before I reach primary school*
*At first beaches, seagulls, wind, and riptides*
*Then the sound of factories and rain on your jacket*
*At five years or less already a secret*
*When leaving I was already planning to go back.*
*Even if I had family all over, not just in northern Italy*
*In Switzerland, in Canada, in Argentina, Australia*
*Blood of my blood, scattered over the map*
*I still hate that immigrants get looked down on*
*And thinking about it, things for me they could've gone worse*
*But mom won the contest, and we're back to Reggio.*
*Like the rain brings the river back to its source*
*Home's where the heart is, not some ordinary place.*

*REFRAIN*
*Got my eyes on the horizon since I was just a boy*
*Dad told me some things that I couldn't understand*
*I get it now, 'cause now it's my destiny*
*I'm the one who writes it, I'm the one who writes it.*

*Got my eyes on the horizon since I was just a boy*
*Dad told me some things that I couldn't understand*
*I get it now because now what I'm living*
*Gives me new reasons for every breath I take.*

*Growing up I had my little victories*
*Did well in school: languages and history*
*First scholarship repayments in the mail*
*A hundred thousand toward the future's cost.*
*And after that, the life of a young Calabrese guy*
*I gave as many punches as I took.*
*At fifteen I was shouting, "The world is mine!"*

*Clashes in squares, fascist symbols, blackjacks and police*
*Saw guns in the schoolyard, blood on the ground*
*Football buddies killed for no reason*
*And I saw guys pretend to be somebody else*
*But their real hometown's always deep inside*
*And the mafiosi painted on the city walls*
*Don't say DC but Casa delle Libertà*
*'95, and here the story doesn't get better*
*At eighteen I get my stuff together and I leave again.*

*Got my eyes on the horizon since I was just a boy*
*Dad told me some things that I couldn't understand*
*I get it now, 'cause now it's my destiny*
*I'm the one who writes it, I'm the one who writes it.*

*Got my eyes on the horizon since I was just a boy*
*Dad told me some things that I couldn't understand*
*I get it now because what I'm living*
*Gives me new reasons for every breath I take.*

*And I find myself in Rome: yes, me the country boy*
*Stuck between going to college and the new millennium*
*Meanwhile a thousand stages, thousand facts, and thousand fights*
*And I kept on looking for the sea between the buildings*
*As for work, I'd say it's more iffy than hourly*
*I wrote, but my rhymes don't make me a salary*
*And now I'm grown and got a mortgage to pay*
*And no money unless I use my brains and my balls.*
*Looking in the mirror: In November I'm 31*
*And still I've never broken or shot anyone*
*I got my own scars and unhappy memories*
*But a sun that's even stronger in the roots*
*And although I'm not one of the winners*

*I know my future and its envious eyes;*
*And I have many more tales than tears to write*
*If she smiles at me, all I can do is live them.*

## 2009–2010

The adventure begins many years later in 2009, with *Sacco o Vanzetti* for Relief Record Europe, a label that has produced some of the most interesting underground Italian rap records and that has formed an overseas partnership with Relief Records NYC. I'm not exactly a novice: I've already released an album with Kalafro (*Solo l'Amore* in 2007, *Resistenza Sonora* will follow in 2011) and four more with Gli Inquilini, a project I started in Rome that lasted from 2002 to 2007. This time, however, it's different.

In general, the moment that I start thinking of a new album is always both difficult and exciting. The risk you face when doing music is quoting yourself, becoming the cover band of yourself, settling for what you can do, not growing. That's why, in my case, it's always about making a clean sweep and unlearning everything I take for granted: I need to think about every next album as my debut album, and if and when I no longer feel this way I'll probably stop making music. Also, to compose an album and to stand on stage alone is a completely different challenge from having a band next to you. I want the album to convey the collective element and the struggles I believe in, but also the more personal element, the lyrical and subjective element. I certainly don't expect it to become a commercial success, but it must be something that truly represents me.

Nazzareno from Relief Records is a pleasant surprise: He is not the stereotype wheeler-dealer label owner, he shows his confidence in me, he respects my artistic choices and uses his connections in the Big Apple to have my album mastered by the sound mixer of artists such as The Roots and Sean Price. As I write this, I can see myself standing in the Brooklyn studio, a small crowd on the other side of the glass, very probably they've never heard a single verse of Italian rap. Just between ourselves, I don't think I made a bad impression. In fact, Dehran of Relief NYC personally oversees the distribution of the album in some circuits in the States.

*"Music Revolution"*
*(from the album by Kento & the Voodoo Brothers* Radici*)*

*The sound's warm like the sun but has the color of night*
*It has a heart like ours but it beats more powerfully*
*Lines on its face, and it has a bastard's smile*
*It looks Death in the face and Death looks away*
*I know very well the answers it can give*
*And I yell on the way like Giovanni has for more than 30 years*
*This is why I speak: for the people who can't speak*
*For those out of time who dream of a vague time*
*Music in the head, but empty hands*
*In headphones at the end of the line at the Piazzale dei Partigiani*
*I write for Reggio and for those who live another day*
*I write another Avvelenata on the walls of the streets*
*I write a note and word, I believe it again*
*I write "Cuba libre" and I don't mean rum and coke*
*And I already said there are a lot of us*
*This is music, a revolution inside your systems*
*I write rhymes and leave sheets on my desk*
*They never sleep and speak to me with the voice of the devil*
*I wake up and every text seems different to me*
*More sarcastic and with plastic dripping from every verse*
*New blood in the arteries of this neighborhood*

*I play strong, I play true, but I don't play well*
*I go around with people who think like me*
*And music saves us, Rock the Casbah like the Clash*
*A circle around the fire is better than a distant stage*
*It's better to lose your voice than to talk softly*
*That's why it's rare that I write past-tense texts*
*Because every day is a struggle, like a cut by Kalafro*
*And on old records the musicians know what it is*
*And why the guitar player sells his soul at the crossroads*
*And on old records the musicians said it*
*That music is the revolution in the mirror.*

According to my personal formulation, there are four important steps in creating music. The first one is study, which may be listening to old records, reading, or simply being inspired by facts or people around us. The second step is the actual writing, it's the moment I set pen to paper. I tend to not anticipate this second phase: The verse must be mature, it must write itself. The Notorious B.I.G., one of the greatest rappers of all time, didn't write at all. He would start off from a concept, a rhyme, or a comparison, and then he built around it: The starting point wasn't necessarily the beginning of a verse, it could be the conclusion or the central focus. He would repeat this concept to himself over and over again and then connect it to the second one and so on. By doing this, his verses became incredibly fluid and consequential. Also the good thing was that when he got to the recording studio he already knew it all by heart and was able to record it in a completely natural and more effective way.

The third moment is when you enter the studio, in many ways the moment of truth. You understand if what you've written holds up against a microphone, in fact you might realize that the clear image you had in your head breaks up and loses its strength the moment it becomes a sound wave on the screen. It's also the moment technical flaws and weaknesses come to the surface: When I was young I was fixated on the precision of the recording and I used to load the verses with overdubs. Now I realize that to record everything in one take, although the sixteenth-notes might be less precise, greatly increases the expression and the impact, so I've simplified everything a great deal. Typically my verses have a take at the beginning, another take with three or four doubles, and that's all. Zero effects, zero tricks. Music and words.

The fourth moment is the live performance, and that's when no half-measures are allowed: It's the favorite moment of many artists, while others, who have a more complex relationship with themselves or with their own image, just can't stand it. There are some emcees who are breathtaking on stage, but when you listen to their record you realize that the writing is actually not that exceptional. Then there are others, especially those who have a more reflexive mood, who write pure poetry but on stage seem cold and distant, although often it's just a bit of shyness. To put it simply: Some love live performance and some aren't that keen on it. I've always been of the first type: Being on stage is a rush of energy, the adrenalin is so much that when I go to bed after a concert I can only get to sleep many hours later.

There's no use denying it: The iconic moment that movies and photos depict the best and that we've all dreamt of as kids is the performance in front of a full room, not the solitary one behind the glass of the recording studio. Music is a loyal friend and lover, and it gives back, amplified, everything you put into it. This is why investing the same love in the writing and the recording that you put into a live performance is the best choice, in my opinion, a rapper can make.

All the books I read and all the records I listen to in a certain sense become part of my songs, part of my way of recording, and of my way of performing in front of an audience. The four moments have become one.

*"What We Aren't"*
*(from the album* Sacco or Vanzetti*)*

*This is the last step, third act of the opera*
*I'm heading toward Chtulhu arm in arm with Lovecraft*
*end in my mind comedies and grotesque dramas*
*of unhappy poets who died young at 30*
*liquid twilight, saga of the minuscule*
*even the heart is a muscle: I don't know anymore if it's right or not*
*and my woman flees among the umbrellas; palpably gone*
*feelings desert me, pour wax over the five senses*
*and the more my head fills up the more I fill notebooks.*
*I speak in the plural because in the name of a generation*
*But I seek the solution on my own.*
*Compasses (with steps) about ourselves, too many turns for so many*
*But I see that sadly it's not a Giotto that is looking for me*
*Unquiet muses at every corner*
*And I ask the page "why don't you speak?" like Michelangelo.*

*REFRAIN*
*We know what we aren't, what we don't want*
*we remain poets who don't speak Italian;*
*it's a cold wind but it will take us far away*
*toward the sudden finale of the twilight of humanity.*

*And if the dream rules the world like the Titan Atlas*
*I will be simultaneously Don Quixote and Cervantes*
*Orlando and troubadour, actor and Rossellini*
*Piero and De André, engineer and Guccini.*
*I bear the signs of millenniums of conflict on my face*
*I carry the flag for the losing team.*
*Even for those who love me I will be dead.*
*Like a Christ who never rose from his tomb.*
*An Adam who had no consciousness of "I"*
*If God's finger had never touched mine*
*A whirligig that spins, but the merry-go-round's stopped*
*Life is an ironic, dramatic charade.*
*I mention again the domino, a tile with letters*
*In part they make art if you know how to place them*
*And we will go a long way leaving no trace*
*We are dice, but with 1 on every side.*

*I'm not a gangster rapper, I'm not a conscious rapper*
*I am, inasmuch as I think, allergic to manners*
*Nihilistic lyric the figures are close to me*
*I'm the double zero in the middle of 2007.*
*The madness of Nietzsche drives me*
*Like Carlos Castaneda I open doors, I seek light.*
*But the shadow remains my companion on my journey*
*I'll draw holy whores like in Caravaggio*
*It represents that darkness I'm drawn to*
*Wilting watches, the insecurity of time.*
*Forgive them lord the flowered maidens.*
*They take me back ten years with a single name.*
*Beyond the limits, the identikit is a limerick*
*Call me Ishmael like the beginning of Moby Dick*
*Curses of the pope, improvised art*
*My way like Sinatra, words by chance, Dada.*

Music, just like any other art form, only reaches its goal the moment it starts to belong to the person listening. Anyone (or almost anyone) who writes will tell you that he or she is writing for him- or herself, but, speaking personally, art for art's sake doesn't satisfy me, I'm not able to imagine it without a further aim. Here you need to shift the focus from the person creating to the person listening. When I write, my ambition is to give the people listening to my music three different levels of listening. The first one is simply the song standing against the background noise, real or metaphysical: The person listening says "he's a good musician, I'm interested." This level reflects the moment I record my music. The second level is when the listener pays attention to the words and to the concept I'm expressing. This level of listening reflects my writing. The third level requires a deeper and more difficult involvement: The person listening wants to expand the subtext and the references that made me write those words. This is the level that reflects my study and inspiration. Making this third level of listening possible is what interests me the most when I write, and naturally it's a goal that is never fully reached. In fact, if we really wanted the listener and the composer to overlap completely we'd need a fourth level, a level in which the music you listen to becomes yours to the point that it inspires you to do something in real life. This, however, is the domain of great artists.

❧

I've gone off track; let's get back to the story. It's the end of 2009: *Sacco o Vanzetti* is released, and for almost two years I tour Italy every weekend to perform it live. It turns out to be a very lucky project because, although it doesn't get to the top of the charts, it is very much liked in the underground scenes, and I discover that there are a lot of people who relate to what I write as much as I do. Many doors open up, starting with the doors of the places that organize live concerts, and to be honest, this is probably the moment my life starts to change.

The best thing that happens to me is that I'm called back to play in places I've been to perhaps a couple of months earlier: It means there's a bond, and I'm not just one of the many who've played there who says thank you and goes off. I realize that, thanks to music, there are places that I can call home even though I wasn't born there. The Forte Prenestino in Rome, the Cantiere in Milan, the CP21 in Livorno are just the first three that come to mind, but the list is long.[4] August 23, the anniversary of the deaths of Sacco and Vanzetti, I'm invited to Torremaggiore, the hometown of Nicola Sacco. Every year his grandson, together with volunteers and activists, organizes a torchlight procession to the grave of the anarchic martyr, and this year my live show accompanies the event. As if this weren't enough, I get an email from Massachusetts: It's the Sacco and Vanzetti Society, saying they're going to broadcast my music during an event that will happen at the same time and at the place of his execution.

*"Sacco or Vanzetti"*
*(from the album* Sacco or Vanzetti*)*

*Voice like light, but if there's no more heat*
*The scream blocks the words, causes eclipses of the sun.*

---

[4] These are examples of self-managed social centers that sprang up in Italy during the 1980s (Trans.).

*Sacco Nicola, hailing from the South*
*Destination death and meantime prison.*
*Inside four walls, even his thoughts locked up.*
*From this enclosure even air can't pass*
*When I'm scared I close my eyes and see the sea,*
*I dream of heaven, my land, and kissing my woman.*
*I dream butterfly wings to pass through the bars,*
*Giant's hands to bend them.*
*I would like strength for a new chapter,*
*If each one of my steps won't lead to the gallows.*
*Anarchist and foreigner, not a killer,*
*even the judge who sealed my fate knows it.*
*And I wrote on the wall, in black letters:*
*"Justice has no place in a system of power."*

*Vanzetti:*
*Voice like a bomb, if the truth we have*
*Breaks the arm held in the Roman salute.*
*Vanzetti Bart, only guilty*
*Of hating the injustice of the system and its rules.*
*Of being Italian, anarchist, emigrant,*
*Unionist, antifascist, militant*
*And my people no longer recall the past*
*With me comes the bill for every wasted second*
*To work illegally like slaves of the master,*
*In an endless line at the immigration offices.*
*Mister Judge, it's all a frame-up!*
*I saw that pen trembling with fear.*
*He wrote the condemnation that is our victory,*
*He wrote our names in the history books,*
*And all of them now need to know:*
*"Justice has no place in a system of power."*

꒛

My activity as a soloist proceeds in parallel with my activity with Kalafro, so I travel back to the Strait of Sicily for the national demonstration against the project for the Messina Strait bridge. The organizers have asked us to play at the end of the march: a wonderful party right at the point where Calabria and Sicily seem to touch. The day doesn't start off well: During the days leading up to the event the authorities have created a tense atmosphere, which is totally uncalled for. They say that crowds of creepy "black blocs" will descend on Villa San Giovanni. The shop owners are told to keep their shutters down, and even the bakers have been instructed to make twice the amount of bread the day before the march, in order to contain the emergency. I've never seen such a concentration of police at the station, not even on the day Mafioso Salvatore Riina[5] appeared on trial in Reggio. But the atmosphere livens up as soon as the march begins: There are songs, colors, flags. We quicken our pace and are the first to arrive in the square where we are supposed to play—we have a sound check to do.

I feel strongly about this day, it's one of the most important struggles of my people. When I walk around up there on stage, I can feel the tension grabbing me by the throat again. The square is totally militarized. Armored vehicles, dozens and dozens of riot-control agents, even the police boats are out patrolling the stretch of sea where usually you'd only see the fishermen's boats going by slowly. Fortunately, the marchers are almost here: Thousands of colors, our comrades, start to give a lively and

---

[5] Former chief of the Sicilian Mafia (Trans.).

more human tone to the menacing evenness of the uniforms and the armored cars.

As often is the case, the concert is preceded by speeches given by the various people promoting the demonstration. We listen with one ear while doing the last checks and making sure everything is in place; we want our show to be perfect despite the persistent noise of helicopters. When Franco Nisticò gets up on stage, however, it's impossible not to pay attention. He is an expert and passionate militant, and he uses nice and simple words: Young and old must fight together to give new hope to our land. He becomes animated while speaking, he becomes ill, he collapses. The people standing there call for an ambulance, and incredibly, despite the deployment of forces, there is no ambulance nearby, nor is it possible to call for one. This is how, on that absurd and hateful day in December, the heart of Franco Nisticò stops.

Silence fills the square. Then the shouts begin: "Murderers!" A group of people from the march break away and move toward the armored vehicles. The charge of the police is abrupt, immediate. Silence falls again. There will be no concert this evening.

The years have gone by, but the Nisticò family have never come to terms with this unacceptable death, obviously. They don't believe (neither do I, for that matter…) that a trial can bring justice, but they want an investigation, and at the end of 2015 a judge sets pen to paper and writes the two words: "negligent homicide." The doctor, who at the moment Franco fell ill was (in the only ambulance equipped with a defibrillator) about three kilometers away, is charged with negligence. As of now, whatever that doctor was thinking no one will ever know, probably not even Franco's children or his many comrades who carried on his work with the same courage and persistence. We do not know if she too fell victim to the collective terror, the tense atmosphere caused by that exaggerated and intimidating militarization. The autopsy revealed that if Franco had received timely assistance, he would still be with his family today.

I don't want to speak of political homicide, I don't want to say that those who terrorized my generous people have blood-stained hands. I don't want to say that Franco Nisticò is the first victim of the Messina Strait bridge. I too, like those who keep his memory alive, want to learn to be persistent, to be courageous, and to remember. We can start by remembering his words: "Facing the many problems of our area, such as hydrogeological instability and those that weigh on the young, like unemployment, we mustn't be divided but stand united. We must fight together to defeat those marching against us. We are our own best hope, young and old. Together we can give hope to the region of Calabria, which has been abandoned by all."

Some months later, we wrote a song titled simply "No Al Ponte" (No to the Bridge), which became the movement's theme song. In the first lines I imagine Ulysses and his warriors returning to confront Scylla and Charybdis, and Franco Nisticò returning to deliver words of unity and hope.

*"No to the Bridge"*
*(from the album by Kalafro* Resistenza Sonora*)*

*It's an electoral spot in view of the local elections*
*A Christmas present for mafiosi and criminals*
*An architect told me that even the project's all wrong*
*Construction sites like slashes in the heart of the Strait*
*Certain people don't get that it will be an apocalypse*

*Others count their profits on the x-axis*
*If Ulysses could come back to this sea, what would he do?*
*He'd take his warriors and fight like they did yesterday!*
*If Franco Nisticò came back, what would he say?*
*"United for the struggle and the good of our people!"*
*I want concrete answers, not rhetoric*
*From Giampilieri to the 106 Jonica*
*Whoever has a voice and a conscience should say it:*
*It's only a monument to the president of the board*
*And all around us there's a million people*
*Who are saying, "No to the bridge," just like this song.*

❧

My journey continues. A weekend in September 2010. As is often the case, I'm on a plane, headed for Trieste-Ronchi dei Legionari. It's the first time I've ever been invited to play in the northern region of Friuli-Venezia Giulia. Also, it's a very special occasion: an important international poetry festival during which I will share the stage with some of the best living Italian authors and with some international giants such as Saul Williams, the poet/rapper/writer who composed some of the best pages of our times. Run DMC t-shirt, Adidas track jacket and rucksack: I wonder what the driver who picks me up at the airport thinks of me; perhaps he was expecting more serious-looking people.

The car takes off for the theater: The flight was delayed and we try to make up for lost time, I have a sound check to do. I enter through the stage door, the theater is immersed in darkness, while on stage Lello Voce, holding a folder, is overseeing rehearsals. Lello is a very successful poet, but above all, as far as I'm concerned, he's the one who brought slam poetry, "clash poetry," to Italy. Digression: If you don't know about this genre... well, I'm giving you a good tip.

*"One Day You Asked Me to Explain to You What It Is"*
*(from the album* Sacco or Vanzetti*)*

*It's the place where the blood runs warm and calm*
*And I rest tired legs after a year of walking*
*It's the moment of silence between words and songs*
*It's like a thousand things, but it's incomparable.*
*It's pure math, precise like algebra*
*But in the midst it beats strong like the drums of Africa.*
*It's Zion for the Rastas, Francesco for my mother,*
*Freedom for my grandfather after a year in the lager.*
*It's the proof that a moment is important,*
*But the drumroll will follow the money, the stone become a diamond.*
*Few words, sheets hanging in the sun*
*So white that they seem to sparkle in that no-color.*
*And as a kid I stared so much at them*
*That if I closed my eyes I still saw the negative.*
*They're the last syllables of every rhyme*
*And the first drawing in my first-grade school book.*
*It's in your smile, on your new dress*
*It's home, and every brick means an hour of work*
*It was Montale when he wrote about lemons,*
*Miles Davis who pulled notes from the solos.*
*Simple and pure, more good than lovely*
*It's faith, but surely it doesn't stop at that ring.*
*And it is born small so that it can sleep in your pocket,*
*Make it red and may it fly high like the flags in the square.*
*It's this and more than I know to say*
*It's round like a record, comes to life via needles.*

*And there's nothing more to understand.*
*You want to stop it? Stop the sun in the middle of its morning rise.*
*And that path is better than any of its meters*
*Just like the word is better than the alphabet*
*Just like music is more than beat and rap*
*Just like "we" are more than I and you.*

It all started in the mid-1980s, in the popular neighborhoods of Chicago. Marc Kelly Smith is a young builder who loves to write poetry and frequents dodgy jazz clubs where, more than half a century earlier, Al Capone and his men used to hang out. Marc can't stand the fact that people seem to be put off by the term "poetry," and he blames it on the way it's taught in schools. Verses must break free from academies, universities, institutions and must be reclaimed by the people. He invents a simple way of renewing its fruition: a race between poets, a clash, which he calls slam. The formula becomes popular, it's a global success, it revolutionizes the approach to poetry as we know it today.

Pay attention: Slam is not about deciding who's the best, it's not about competing, winning, defeating the adversary. The challenge is only an excuse to exchange verses, see how they work when read out loud, to understand what reaches the audience and what doesn't. Some authors write wonderful poetry, but they can't deliver it as well, and they're always the first to be defeated. There are others who write things that are not as good, but they compensate with their presence on stage. Competition only makes the reading more dramatic and thrilling: The audience is the only jury to decide who stays and who goes home.

In the meantime, hip-hop is spreading in the United States, and soon it crosses over and infects slam poetry. The rules are not that different from those of our freestyle battle, the focus is on words but also on dramatic presence, on the ability to interpret words live. Clearly the fact that one knows that these words will be interpreted live changes also the technique and the intention of writing.

Thirty years after these legendary events, I am in the foyer of a large concert hall in Rome, along with Marc Kelly Smith. I was master of ceremonies for the slam that has just ended. He is the special guest of the evening and his show was extraordinary, as always. I try to imagine, not without a touch of envy, the emotions he went through when he made his debut. I wonder what it's like to invent an original literary/performative genre, I wonder whether he's ever regretted turning down big contracts and opportunities to stay loyal to the original spirit of those old jazz clubs in Chicago.

But back on that September day in Friuli I still hadn't met Marc and had never been on a slam poetry stage. On that day in front of me I see Lello Voce, whom I know only because he's famous, and a bunch of technicians busily mounting the set. I pause in the darkness to observe the scene, waiting for my turn to do a sound check. But Lello turns round, points at me, and goes, "You're Kento!" I smile, he extends his hand and pulls me up on stage. That moment I know we'll become friends.

From that day I start to be invited to poetry events quite regularly, I always feel like I'm not supposed to be there. I find myself passing the microphone to very important authors: guys who are in school textbooks, who translate Sappho and Beckett, who knew Pasolini and Alda Merini when my parents were still in high-school. My only weapon is nerve and I decide to use it the best I can. I steal what I can, I try to improve my technique and my expression. I realize that, if it's true that rappers are a category of crazy, misanthropic, egotistical people, often poets are not very different, and this discovery somehow makes them more human and closer to me. I decide to take part in slams. Not many are expecting a rapper to show up: I'm quite successful, I often win, even against writers who are probably better than me.

"He'll Have Your Eyes"
(*from the album* Sacco or Vanzetti)

*I write figures in pencil while I count bank notes*
*September already in the South, night blue as notes*
*In the club I've got dancers, bartenders, bluesmen, and jazzmen*
*And I serve teacups filled to the brim with good whisky*
*Tequila and weed from Tijuana, cognac from France, Cohibas from*
*     Havana*
*I hate the feds but the local cops*
*Here stand guard like officials at a club*
*For which the money's never meagre*
*I smile like the devil at my poker table*
*So even if I paid out, there's no problem*
*Four million in the bank like four aces in the hand*
*Snuck in like in a ship's hold*
*Ten years and a thousand dramas later, in my hand I have an empire*
*And don't push back, the Italian means business*
*This country is mine, don't call me a foreigner.*

*It's quiet in the bar, just to see her come in*
*Hits me like a right hook in the solar plexus.*
*Dressed in white silk and with emerald eyes*

*I don't speak but I return her hot glances*
*No one knows her or can guess who she is*
*None of these men can say "She's mine"*
*And the chief of police is quiet*
*Because in those eyes he sees fire and anarchy.*
*But all this silence makes me nervous and I can't take it*
*I'm in charge here and the only god is the dollar!*
*It's up to me to explain it to all these people*
*Who's right here, it's not always the customer*
*And I come up to this unknown girl*
*Smiling, "Please, Miss, have a seat"*
*I gesture to the bar: two glasses of the best stuff*
*And then I play my hand like when it rains outside.*

*And in the place there's no sound, no note*
*Every candle's blown out, every bottle's empty*
*Spider webs on the walls like frescoes*
*I look people in the eyes and see skulls*
*My entire present seems so distant*
*Only she remains, beautiful and elegant*
*She smiles and says nothing, she's still sitting there*
*But now she knows that I recognize her*
*A thousand times she's passed me by while I drove, exhausted,*
*Or when I bust the house*
*A thousand times she's taken me and let me go*
*Like the one who promises to return*
*And another thousand times I've called her in vain*
*And I spat bile suffering from being left*
*But now she is here and I say, "OK, here we are*
*Don't tell me where we're going, but hold my hand."*

*Read me the future in the cards*
*Or in the depths of broken cups*

*Death will come, and he'll have your eyes*
*And I don't know where or when*
*But I know I'm waiting for death*
*Who has the same gaze as you.*

The slam movement grows in Italy, it spreads. Lello Voce, together with a group of visionaries, decides it's time to bring local scenes together that very often don't even talk to each other or know about each other. The Italian League of Slam Poetry (LIPS) is born and with it the first national championship, with qualifying rounds held locally and a national final, which allows the winners to travel abroad to compete at a European and international level. Again: The aim is not to compete, the challenge is simply a way of bringing poetry closer to its audience, to the people. I am invited to become a member of the governing council of LIPS, and with my usual bravura, I accept. The adventure of slam poetry in Italy is still unfolding, and no one knows where it will take us.

# 2011–2013

2011: It's time to go south again. *Resistenza Sonora* is released, the most important work of my band, Kalafro. A lot is happening in Reggio Calabria, and the main actor in these events is the youngest and most courageous member of the band, Simone, also called Mad Simon. Even before the record is out, when there is still no particular need to promote it, he invents a new strategy to launch our message and make it heard.

He lives near the Aragonese Castle, the only ancient building in Reggio Calabria that has withstood the earthquakes and the other natural and human disasters of the last centuries. The castle is one of the undisputed symbols of the city. Simone gets hold of a very powerful projector, I don't know where he gets it, and hides it on a balcony, and he starts to project enormous letters on the walls of the castle. "NO" the first night, "TO" the second one, and finally "THE 'NDRANGHETA" to complete the message. He signs the message with our name to lay claim to it and so it's not left anonymous.

It's a clear November day, the kind we often enjoy in the South. You can still sit outside in the evening, the air is fresh; the projection is clear, and it shines out from the dark of the night, the outlines are sharp, it could be painted. The castle, like all castles, is built on the highest part of the city, so the message dominates the main street, the waterfront, and the places of power.

We obviously never asked for any permission. People are curious, they stop and look, some police patrols try to figure out where the light is coming from. People share the message on social media by the hundreds. The press reports on it, and a nice gallery of images documenting the whole operation appears in the newspaper *La Repubblica*. The piece is picked up by a bunch of other national outlets. Mission accomplished: The "NO TO THE 'NDRANGHETA" has made the rounds of Italy. Simone takes the projector apart and lets out a sigh of relief: No one ever discovered on which balcony it was placed, and if someone did then they must be like-minded, as no one tries to get us into trouble.

*"Dear Brother"*
*(from the album by Kento & the Voodoo Brothers* Radici*)*

*I don't believe in this state, today like yesterday*
*In carved stones and police uniforms*
*Violence is for them, we're not alike*
*Old cities, new busts in the social centers*
*And your gold can't buy our blood*
*Dead from work, the same red flowers on the coffins*
*It's heard in Rosarno and in Sicily, you hear it all over the South*
*In Val di Susa and in the ice of ThyssenKrupp*
*When I write the ink pierces the page*
*The future is poetry, the fantasy of whoever imagines it*
*after 20 years same fight, same stage*
*fists up and keffiyeh over my face like in '94*
*And whoever doesn't shout either has no voice or else has no faith*
*But the capital is always the same: it's always in bad faith*
*I make music and I know that tomorrow*
*is in the lines on the face and the calluses of the hands.*

ৎ

Some months later a priest gets in touch with us, don Mario. He is a streetwise priest, there are only a few left, the kind that don Gallo and don Puglisi would have liked. He asks us to play in his neighborhood, Piscopio, a village in the district of Vibo Valentia where a bloody feud had broken out in those days. I'm already booked for that evening, but his request is too important to refuse, and the band arranges things so we can go and play. It's October 1, 2011, a Saturday. The concert means a lot, for many reasons, perhaps too many for a group of boys who play in a band. As if that weren't enough, it's the feast of St. Michael the Archangel, the celestial army general that the Mafia bosses believe is their patron and protector.

Piscopio is in one of those corners of Calabria that is full of history, where the names of every outcropping and every stream bear the noble sound of ancient Greek. The dialect is sweeter and more melodic than in other places: According to a legend the inhabitants of this land inherited their inflections from the singing of the mermaid Lisia, a maidservant of the goddess Persephone.

That evening, however, the bewitching songs of the mermaids of the past cannot be heard. The atmosphere is surreal; some of the organizers seem to be on the point of bursting into tears. We have been announced by a phone call from the marshal of the Carabinieri, and the square is swarming with police. Officers, armored vehicles, plainclothes policemen, no one else. The posters have been torn down, and the order has been given in the nearby towns to stay away, no matter what. Two bullets were found in the church, under the statue of St. Michael. A dejected don Mario doesn't even leave his home. A cocky young boy comes up to us: "How much is the priest paying you? Make sure he pays well...." No one smiles. All four wheels of the priest's car have been slashed. The sound system for the concert is nowhere to be seen, although the service was pre-booked. The organizers call all the suppliers they can think of, then all the ones in the phone directory, but it's useless: No one is willing to take the risk of providing the speakers, the microphones, the mixer.

We could improvise an unplugged concert: We have guitars and djembes, anything is better than silence. But one glance at the organizers is enough to make it clear that it's out of the question. Our van goes to a different place every night; these people live here. The event is canceled.

The rumors inevitably spread. Starting the next day, we are overwhelmed with phone calls and emails. The newspaper headlines: "The 'Ndrangheta calls off the Kalafro concert." Roy Paci writes a nice piece in solidarity and is imitated by a large part of the music scene in the South. The most important TV and radio stations would like to interview us, even the ones that ignored our music until yesterday. We give them a stiff "No comment." We have a record to promote: It would be easy to get visibility by taking advantage of a dramatic event that isn't ours. We tell the journalists to interview the real fighters: don Mario and the activists of our region, the people who toil here every day.

Years have gone by now, and I decided to put this story down on paper so it will be remembered and because I think that those directly involved are no longer at risk. There are some details I feel like omitting, because we were asked to at the time and I know how strong the memory of my fellow countrymen is, for better or for worse; anyway, those aren't central elements to the story.

The following evening, October 2, 2011, Amedeo Minghi held his concert at Piscopio and had no trouble at all.

*"Struggle"*
*(from the album by Kalafro* Resistenza Sonora*)*

Look around you and you'll see why I fight
I have battle plans in my rhymebook, assault techniques
shoes on the pavement and eyes on the cobalt blue
I need to dream twice as much because some don't dream at all
Reggio Calabria city and you say you understand us
but respect costs a lot and a bullet's two cents
That's why every rhyme is hot like the Sahara
and the sound stops the villain's bullet in the air when he shoots
I hit hard without using a shotgun
if you're behind me you hear the echo all across Italy
I raise the volume so the bass shakes the walls
Kento gives voice to the revolt of 2010.
And every note resounds like a bomb
Every rhyme breaks a rule because it counterinforms
With these words I destroy the bridge over the Strait
I burn the Mafia money they got for project signatures
If men of honor are the first among the villains
who have the blood of the honest on their hands, here there's no tomor-
    row
I keep separate journalism from the news
I keep separate judge, verdict, and justice …
And what they've taken from us won't come back
no matter how many candles for the Madonna my grandmother's lit
Money makes money, hunger makes hunger
If I die bring a bud to smoke and pour wine in the sea
If I survive to fight another day
every word will be revolution for those who listen
What you hear if you turn off the news
is Babylon crumbling under the weight of its own evil.

Another inland town in Calabria, another surreal scene: We've been invited to play by a local committee for public water. The event is organized to protest the privatization of this indispensable resource but also to protest the many unauthorized tap-ins and the abuses of the territory. It's a summer evening, we're in the main square, the windows of the houses are open. The atmosphere is tense and the square is empty. The sound technician and the organizers look desolately at one another, the small audience huddles together close to the stage. One of the rules of live performances is that the people who come shouldn't be penalized because of those who don't, and the concert must be energetic, powerful, loaded. We raise our voices, to break the gray sheet of silence, fifteen people make the noise of one hundred, and it winds up in a crowd of smiles and photos. At this point something absurd happens. Little by little the inhabitants of the town come out from their homes and wander toward the small stand where our CDs are on sale. They smile and compliment us in quiet tones; they buy the CD and go back home. The windows were left open not only to let the fresh air in, but also to listen to us. Someone had "discouraged" people from attending the concert, but the people wanted to thank us and support us anyway. It makes us happy: A concert only lasts one evening, but a record is a seed that can be listened to thousands of times and generate unexpected flowers. By the time we leave, the CDs are all sold out.

Our trusted sound technician, Maurizio, accompanies us throughout the tour. He's a pretty good rapper himself, a filmmaker and many other things. He is always doing something: He organizes parties, produces albums, records, mixes. But, as the people where I'm from would say, Maurizio has a bad habit: He can't keep quiet. As soon as he feels something isn't right he pops off. Perhaps he doesn't think things through enough, like the time when we'd just finished recording our album and he hung a sign on the door of the studio in Reggio that read: "Sound Resistance underway in this studio: The 'Ndrangheta is not welcome." The following morning the door had been forced open and the studio was full of trash. On another occasion he was playing in a club frequented by "respectable" people celebrating the birthday of a mob soldier. They sat down and started ordering bottles for thousands of euros, draining them. It got late, the party came to an end, and Maurizio unplugged his equipment. They asked for more music but he told them it was late, everyone had left, and he'd already loaded half of his gear on the truck. He's a big guy, and he didn't like the way they were trying to make him play. They were all excited because of the wine, like a pack of animals, and wouldn't take no as an answer. He got beaten up, but he knows well it could have been worse.

Fires, burglaries, sabotages: six episodes of intimidation in three years. He is guilty of making music and of never keeping his mouth shut. The last event, the worst, happened in January 2013, when he found five bullets in his car. He reacted the way we thought he would: He went into the studio, wrote a song to denounce what had happened, and filmed a video clip. When I spoke to him, he told me he was tired, that he was thinking of going up north, where a part of his family lives, where he could work in peace, and even make more money. The years have gone by and Maurizio is still in Reggio, fighting.

*"Sonic Resistance"*
*(from the album by Kalafro* Resistenza Sonora*)*

*It's sonic resistance on the street and on the scene,*
*I write and counterinform against the chloroform of the system.*
*We fight, the sound tears off the masks*
*and three quarters of the music market has no character.*
*New warriors, brigands like yesterday's,*
*I don't want a boss, but neither cops nor vigilantes:*
*battles in the street like in Santa Clara*
*and a Guevara T-shirt is worth only what you sweated.*
*Password like pass the joint,*
*give a history lesson to the "death to cowards";*
*trains are still running to Reggio Calabria*
*and every massacre that gets covered up makes our anger sharper.*
*Dedicated to the internal roots*
*to those who've been in the North 30 years and never lost their accent:*
*revolution in my every word*
*and in the people who play it… Sonic Resistance.*

&

In the meantime, we launch a new project. We meet at the 'Ndrangheta Museum, a villa confiscated from the criminal organization that has become an important center for documentation on the Mafia. The route we take by car makes me reflect on the good and bad things of my city. The journey takes about half an hour: My house is on the northern outskirts, where the strait seems to touch Sicily, while the museum is on the top of a hill that overlooks the southern outskirts. The natural scenery is breathtaking: We are standing in the exact point where the view opens up in the direction of Catania, on our left the majestic outline of

Mount Etna, while to our right the sea is a blue slash separating the island from the continent. Around the villa the road makes a series of hairpin bends and there are few buildings: A person approaching would inevitably be noticed, and it's natural to think that whoever built it had in mind the strategic position in addition to the view. The only reference point nearby is a soccer school called Ciccio Cozza, after the captain of the Reggina who took the team to the Serie A. The guys from the museum erect road signs on many occasions, but the signs don't last long, so they have given up, telling people who don't know the way to ask for the Soccer School Ciccio Cozza. Everybody knows where that is, and everyone gives the information very kindly and in great detail.

On entering the villa visitors are impressed by the invisible bunker, hidden under the floor of the kitchen, and by the luxurious bathrooms with large whirlpool tubs; there are thousands of activities to be discovered. This time, however, the challenge is on a musical level.

We are talking about the tarantella, the most popular folk music in Southern Italy, also defined as "stolen tempo" because of its irregular rhythm. Over the course of the years, the criminal organization has tried to claim some kind of possession of the Calabrian tarantella. The order with which people dancing enter and the role played by the dance leader sometimes reflect the hierarchy of the clans, and nowadays during some weddings the tarantella is not even played, because it's likely that the guests, having had too much to drink, will start fighting over the roles in the dance. If this seems archaic to you, or unbelievable, just keep in mind that the last reported episode of intimidation in which an anti-mafia activist was forced to dance in a *ruota* (in the center of a circle of people) in Reggio was in 2014. The Calabrian tarantella is also the genre that is most used to accompany the lyrics of Mafia songs, which praise the local bosses and the pseudo-values of the mob.

These songs, although unusual in terms of content, are often extremely effective from a narrative point of view, their delivery and immediacy in no way inferior to that of the best rap in New York. The graphic design of CDs of this music leaves little to the imagination: outlines of hanged men with the writing "This is what happens to those who talk," blood, Bible verses, chains—the whole imagery. It's a terrible weapon in the hands of the enemy, and our job is to try and defuse it. First of all, we agree, stolen tempo is not—and never should be—considered a criminal genre. Secondly, we must unmask the hateful messages that the Mafia songs contain. We must reclaim the Calabrian tarantella. Tempo Rubato alla 'Ndrangheta[6] is born.

This project involves many activities. We start with a series of workshops held in middle schools, during which our Simone works side by side with teachers and experts. The kids study the Mafia songs, they decode them, they change them, they turn them around. Our band, the Kalafro, has its own tarantella: a song called "The Collective Ballad." We shoot a video with the students. The whole experience becomes a documentary that gets presented at a national film competition for kids and wins first prize, a golden kite. We have retaken our "stolen tempo."

The workshops continue and start to bother the "Mafia singers," and this is where the story becomes grotesque. It would be funny, if it weren't so dramatic. It's 2014: The news that the work with the kids in the schools is continuing reaches two big shots from this kind of music, a singer

---

[6] Stolen Tempo from the 'Ndrangheta (Trans.).

and a producer; some say they have been informed by some teachers. They both live in Germany, where they are incredibly successful. They get on a plane, they land in Reggio, rent a large car, and drive up to the top of the hill to the 'Ndrangheta Museum. With a tone and attitude that can easily be imagined, they demand respect and money. They have the nerve to speak of royalties, of a "compensation" they are owed because of the damage caused by the workshops with the kids. Simone and the others don't tolerate any of this, they report the intimidation and give the names of the two guys. Andrea Galli writes in the newspaper *Corriere della Sera:* "For the first time a prosecutor in Calabria will take a hard look at the phenomenon of business, performance and rationalization, encoded messages in the texts, and territorial control. The investigations may go deep, and it is bothering the clans, who by now consider this type of music as sacred as the family: for them it is inviolate." Proceedings are still under way, and who knows how it will end?

*"Stalingrad"*
*(from the album* Sacco or Vanzetti*)*

*Anxiety that kills us, and don't tell me to smile*
*Ask me to fight, because fighting is living.*
*I don't believe in the sirens of success*
*I'm not the next no one, I am the first myself.*
*And if the victim is music and the accusation is murder*
*I kill the radio stars, like video.*
*I paint with verses because rap that I move forward*
*Soils black robes and white collars with red.*
*And I don't give a fuck if you have a gun, powder in the packet*
*the emcees you name are men without pisciola*

Revolution in my every word
And in whoever takes it from Milano to Palermo and isn't Raul Bova.
Evolution continues like a writer with lettering
I push those with the ideas, not the ones who say they have them.
And if this is a war, who decides who wins?
Music, the last trench of Stalingrad.

REFRAIN
For the one who knows it's a war and it's an everyday struggle
For the one who will resist by all means necessary
For the one who is outside fashion and the stadiums
Music is the last trench of Stalingrad.

And there's a lot of us, and we're not cynical
I look ahead, in the sky with diamonds like Lucy
Alarms sound rebels run down your Blackberry
I sing love with pain in my heart like Otis Redding
Blood on my rhyme book, with a million pages
And I don't change a word because some manager told me to
Fashion etiquette doesn't value my project
My rhymes don't pay into it, so they are priceless.
A rapper knows an uncertain work is better
Than sucking up for a contract and radio time
And a rapper knows it will always go badly
If the music industry is slave to money.
Without nation or flag if it is from this Italy,
We are warriors of the night and there's no Coney Island.
There's just resisting by any means necessary
Music, last trench of Stalingrad.

REFRAIN
Music is a high wire, it's a microphone wire
It's fire, play, outburst, pogo, it's the philosopher's logos.

*And what classifies it conforms it*
*The thing that covers the Vatican's lies with the Magnificat.*
*Music asked me for a hundred and gave me a thousand in exchange*
*Because the sold one is mute, not only the tired one*
*A thousand songs and cutaways on the palimpsests*
*And seven notes like flowers on the tombs of Sacco and Vanzetti.*
*Real music goes beyond words*
*It's like high voltage, sometimes if you touch it you die.*
*It goes beyond instrument, tempo, sample*
*The one who plays it smiling is terribly serious*
*It's a supreme love like John Coltrane*
*It doesn't have faith in the Re Mida or in the hit parade beats.*
*I'm staying outside fashion and the stadium*
*Music is the last trench of Stalingrad.*

∽

Touring with Kalafro is always an incredible experience, one way or another. The idea of mixing rap and reggae and folk music has allowed us to reach a very diverse audience, so one evening we play in a big social center in Milan, and the following evening at a feast honoring a patron saint of the smallest village in Calabria. The minivan with the writing "RESISTENZA SONORA" on the side endures the kilometers up and down Italy. On one occasion, in the mountains in Calabria, we find the organizers of the concert waiting for us just outside the town with a fleet of Ape Piaggio vehicles: The streets are too narrow and cars can't get through. We put all our equipment in the three-wheelers, which are in perfect state and brand new, and discover that these crazy guys have even changed the motors on them so they can drive uphill at full speed, going 'round the curves on two wheels. We get to the building where the concert is going to be held unharmed, luckily, but yellow with fright and carsickness.

On another occasion we are traveling to another small inland town, and we decide, feeling confident in the technology of the third millennium, to use the navigation system on our smartphones. The problem is that the connection in the valleys of the Calabrian Apennines is not very collaborative, so we are forced to make our way on the provincial roads. When we arrive it's terribly late, the feast of the patron saint is under way, the streets are closed off and swarming with people: Literally the entire population of the town is in the streets. The air is filled with the distinctive smell of crunchy almonds and of chickpeas roasted in sand as well as by the sharp sound of the air rifles doing target shooting. The neon lights of the stands give a fluorescent reflection to the toys, to the raffle prize wheel, and to goldfish on sale inside their individual little tanks. The only traffic warden, in full uniform, removes the barrier and walks in front of our van, the crowd opening up before us. The scene is made even more surreal by the fact that someone recognizes us — or perhaps they think we are real singers — and starts to clap. I can't help it, and I start to wave like the pope from the backseat, ignoring the guy next to me who digs his elbow into my ribs. It's a sort of miniature Disneyland (the right scale for us), and I can't help but play a role myself.

The time comes to present the album in the big cities of Central and Northern Italy. In Rome the association DaSud organizes a fantastic evening. We are particularly fond of them, so much so that we titled the intro to the album *Da Sud*. Their battles have always been ours, and it's the period of the publication *Bloodstained Oranges: The Rosarno Dossier*, which denounces the inhumane situation in Rosarno.

The club is in San Lorenzo, the student neighborhood of Radio Onda Rossa and of the occupations. It fills up, everyone sings our songs, we feel at home.

Still in the capital, I take a turn doing a round of interviews: Saxa Rubra, Radio1, RaiNews24, Tg2. This channel broadcasts the program everyone is waiting for; all our friends and relatives are tuned in and ready. My mother would probably like me to wear a shirt, but I feel comfortable wearing my usual gray hoodie, no logo, bought on sale in New York some months earlier. As soon as I enter the newsroom I can sense the atmosphere is strange. The journalist makes me wait a long time, and then she explains to me—with a long-winded circumlocution—that they have listened carefully to the songs and are not sure they can broadcast them. The incriminating passage is a verse of "Resistenza Sonora" where I speak of a "street battle," which is interpreted as an incitement to violence. I am taken completely by surprise: They were the ones who got in touch with us; haven't they listened to our music? Also, it's clear that when I speak about *weapons* and *battles* I'm talking about culture and social struggles, not placing bombs on street corners. She asks me, "What if a kid listening to you misinterprets your words and decides to go get a pistol?" I'm about to answer back when I meet the eloquent gaze of Luca, our press officer. I say, in the most polite way possible, that I believe the real incitement to violence on TV is the disproportionate and morbid attention that some news programs give to episodes of crime, which glorify the executioner and the avenger and play with the fear of immigrants and of people who might seem different. Not my songs. I stick my pass in the turnstile and leave the complex of Saxa Rubra. I head toward the gloomy station where the trains to the center leave; it's actually only a small platform covered in writings and empty beer bottles. Obviously the interview is never aired. Some time later, however, an episode of *Tg2 Dossier* dedicated to the riots in Reggio is broadcast: Our music, taken out of context and emptied of its true meaning, is used as a soundtrack for the 1970 revolt, during which the fascist motto "Boia chi molla" (death to traitors) echoed through the streets.

*"Roots Music"*
*(from the album by Kento & the Voodoo Brothers* **Radici***)*

*The roots of my sound are in popular song*
*History written with blood on the blades of swords*
*Roots music, the outcasts sing it*
*With negative balance in the bank and just fists in pocket*
*And the invaders imposed their saints on us*
*With our bread in their mouths they called us brigands*
*The South of the world has more blues than Robert Johnson*
*And the future is ours only if I remember*
*Because out of fury is born a new awareness*
*And here old ruins are new foundations*
*I speak in dialect with respect for our ancestors*
*We live years apart but I know that we are the same*
*I know that we are rock from Magna Grecia*
*We are paper for poetry as opposed to paper for money*
*And it's not nostalgia for roots*
*It's called Life, belonging, blood, love, scars.*

*I sing the invisible saga of every son of Hannibal*
*And the bitterness in the rhymes is the old evil of living*
*We are defeated, the migrants, the bastards*
*The state murders but says to us, "Stay calm"*

*If that were true the sun would be enough*
*But that song says "die a brigand"*
*If there were a god he'd have my grandfather's eyes*
*But he wouldn't have the heart to remember about it every day*
*Colonialism changes its face, not its essence*
*Today it has the same weapon and the money from every bank*
*I have the books of philosophers, the volume of microphones*
*And in my accent the voices of a hundred peoples*
*I have always chosen and always the wrong side*
*And the record isn't beautiful but it weighs a ton*
*Another day with the struggle and the memory*
*Another push from below on the wheel of history.*

The Milan concert is coming up. We're going to play in a social center run by young and very young activists: Many girls, a lot of middle-school students. The name is Cantiere, and it's an incredible place. Some decades ago, the elegant building opposite the headquarters of the newspaper *Sole24Ore* used to house the Derby Club, a historic club where musicians such as Coltrane and Quincy Jones played and where Enzo Jannacci, Giorgio Gaber, and Mina Mastroianni were regulars. Even Bettino Craxi the politician could be seen here, but also legendary criminals Francis Turatello and Luciano Lutring—they say Lutring had to escaped the police more than once by climbing out the window. The place was left unoccupied and abandoned for years, some say there is a dispute over the ownership. When the collective of the Cantiere occupied it everyone was happy to see the place come to life again. Even the comedy duo Cochi e Renato (Renato Pozzetto and Cochi Ponzoni) performed for free on its tenth birthday, and they hadn't done anything together for years.

The night of our concert, expectations are high. The organizers have printed a lot of posters, and they put them up at the train stop used by the commuters who come in from the hinterland. The posters, however, don't last long. Every evening the comrades do the rounds to put them up, and every morning they find they've been torn down. No one really pays attention at first, in every city there are those who like to play these tricks, for no reason. The concert is scheduled to take place on a Saturday. Wednesday evening a group of two boys and two girls decide, perhaps naively, that the moment has come to go and put the posters up in a neighborhood on the edge of the city, where there is a concentration of people from Calabria. They imagine that all the inhabitants of the area will enjoy listening to a band that represents their region and its desire for redemption. They are wrong.

As soon as they get the buckets and glue out, they are approached by a small group of men, their accent is unquestionably Calabrian. They speak in a kind tone of voice, they are carrying tools, they look like builders or factory workers. They ask to see the posters, their tone of voice changes. They hold the posters up and rip them to pieces. "This band is a bunch of liars," "they have no respect," and most importantly, "these people are linked to the groups raising hell over the orange trade in Rosarno." The tools now look like sinister weapons in their hands. "Get out of here."

Thursday morning I get a phone call from the social center: They're worried. They're thinking of organizing reinforced security for the concert, they ask me who our enemies in the Lombardia region are. "The same as yours," I answer. I reassure them: I've seen this happen before and I know that when a crowd gathers on the evening of the concert nothing will happen, nobody will come knocking on the door to make a scene. Just to be sure, I call all the friends who've told me they'll be there and suggest they come as a group. The evening is a real success. So much for the guys who wanted us to call it off!

Some time later, the street-art group Volkswriterz decorates the whole façade of the Cantiere. The "people's writers" are a collective of artists I really admire, and they decided to reciprocate this admiration by painting a portrait of me on the wall. Today if you pass by the ex Derby Club not only do you meet the ghost of Coltrane but also a cosmonaut/superhero Kento, obviously with a microphone in hand.

*"H.I.P. H.O.P. (I HAVE POWERFUL IDEAS, I HAVE CLEAR OBJECTIVES)"*
*(from the album by Kento & the Voodoo Brothers* Da Sud*)*

*Today is no longer the day to be indecisive*
*I have powerful ideas, I have clear objectives*
*As long as the ruling class makes its own crises*
*I have powerful ideas, I have clear objectives*

*For whoever judges art by its contracts and by how many hear it*
*Hip-hop is completely alive, it's you who are dead*
*In the street there's a ferment from those you don't want to deal with*
*Culture and resistance between charges and teargas*
*Our freedom is need on my page*
*Antifa, written in huge letters by Partizan*
*Who controls panic has the iron grip*
*To write and fight here as an organic intellectual*
*In the refugee camps B-boys on the cement*
*Smash the Wall, Reggio-Palestina, the crew I represent*

*From Rosarno to Valsusa what does the movement listen to*
*I bring love and rap live to every location of the struggle*
*Too many disco emcees, too many keyboard gangstas*
*What matters really is what's under the New Era*
*This love isn't bought, the curses and the smiles*
*I have powerful ideas, I have precise objectives*
*This scene is only a scene so as to put buffoons on the web.*
*In the real gangsta quarters they do what you write*
*Emcee bathes the microphone in the fire of a Molotov*
*And a rapper will be able to give voice to a people*
*Don't tell me "they're great" if they have idiotic lyrics:*
*Is this lyric hardcore or just to tell us how much you fuck?*
*The market sponsors the rapper who promotes it*
*But if the substance is missing you will smoke only Rizlas*
*This is dedicated to those who sometimes think of quitting*
*Fight what we are for the sake of what we could be*
*If someone used to say the sky's the limit*
*The gold is underground, not at the top of the charts*
*And I hope that someday, listening again to our records*
*We won't say that we had the means and we didn't see them*
*We won't be puppets anymore, no longer alone or divided*
*With powerful ideas and clear objectives.*

૭

In the meantime, in Reggio, Kalafro have become local celebrities. Kids stop us in the street, some ask to have their picture taken with me. They're not all militants or involved in politics: The album also contains light pieces, songs about love, dance tracks. We try to write music we can fully identify with and avoid saying stupid things also when speaking about less serious issues.

We start to pay attention to things we hadn't really noticed before: If we know that a certain ice-cream shop has ties to the 'Ndrangheta, we go somewhere else. The requests for concerts increase: A large beach resort calls us, it's a very fashionable place, and offers to pay very well. They're not interested in what our message is but in the fact that somehow we are the group of the moment, and they think they'll fill the place. We ask around and soon find out that the resort is owned by people who are connected to an influential "family." We turn down the offer, though we can't stop them from playing our most upbeat and least political pieces almost every evening. The sound follows us, derisively, when we walk along that stretch of beach, and our music sounds really alien to us.

On another occasion we are invited to play at a large gathering dedicated to tuning, the art of modifying cars. The event has no social value, but there's a lot of money involved and after all, there's no harm in adding alloy wheels and subwoofers to cars, right? We feel a bit out of context but the concert goes well, and people dance and have fun. Ciccio Svelo listens from a corner, he looks at us, chuckling and drinking a bottle of wine. He's a lawyer, a comrade, he's completely crazy, and he was one of the first people to believe in our music. Ciccio is anything but a tranquil person, and he knows that with us he's free to do whatever he wants. At the end of the concert there's a problem with the payment: The organizers say we'd agreed to something different, and they try to impose another price. We remain very calm: Musicians have these kinds of problems all the time, and there's almost always a solution.

At that moment, however, our improbable savior comes to our rescue. Nobody asked him to, but the drunk angel Ciccio Svelo intervenes in the discussion, in a sneering tone directed at the organizer who thinks he is a hot shot, and jokingly threatens to call his "mates from San Luca." The atmosphere becomes tense immediately. For once we are not able to bring the discussion back to a normal tone. We go home with little money and our tail between our legs, but fortunately there are no other consequences. I say goodbye to Ciccio Svelo and in a friendly manner I tell him to get lost. He has no clue he's made such a mess, he's happy and drunk and is dancing under the trees in the square. This is the last memory I have of him: He died only a few weeks later, age forty-eight, leaving a marvelous archive of books, records, and materials documenting his vast intellect, his insatiable curiosity, and his complete refusal to conform to anything. Today an organization that offers free legal advice for the homeless or victims of any type of injustice bears his name.

❧

As I write this, I realize that the tales of the living are intertwined with the tales of the dead. Christmas evening 2011 comes to mind: The horrible sleet that falls in the Sila region causes an accident that takes the lives of a group of very young rappers and lovers of our music. The whole town of San Giovanni in Fiore gathers around the family and the closest friends. The idea is born of organizing a memorial concert to be held every year: They call it As They Like. I remember the first edition, in 2012. I can see myself engulfed by the palpable emotion of thousands of people gathered in this large open-air amphitheater. The breeze blows in the direction of the deep valley that opens up about ten meters beyond. I've been staring into it all afternoon, thinking about what I'm going to say at the beginning of the concert. Now that it's dark I can only imagine the large void and the town perched on the other side of the crest. I walk on stage and take the microphone. There is complete silence. I have no memory of what I said. But I can still feel the tension growing and then exploding. I remember the people dancing and jumping, the older people off to one side, the same spark in their eyes. Since that summer not only has the memory not faded, but As They Like has become an increasingly important and large event, with international artists and people traveling hundreds of kilometers to climb up the Sila to take part. They called me back and invited me to play again, this time with the rest of the band, and I realized that the August 2012 concert had stayed in all our hearts, not just mine.

*"Brigands"*
*(from the album by Kalafro* Resistenza Sonora)

*This is truth, the post's high as De La,*
*lyrical Guernica, Apocalypse my canvas,*
*what faith, today that no one is safe anymore,*
*Paper burns, Fahrenheit 451.*
*Reggio Calabria where it's almost always summer,*
*where many bullets fly but hardly any bullshit.*
*The youth that stays thinks only of itself*
*and in the shit smokes more grass than Dr. Dre,*
*yeah, they shout because there's no one to hear*
*and they push hard because they're dying of hunger.*
*Ours are the only gazes that don't change,*
*I listen to Bob singing "War inna Babylon."*
*We fight like we've always done,*
*fists up and keffiah over the face like in '94,*

*sheets with our thoughts, dreams, and desires,*
*sorry, but I don't sing your National Anthem.*

*If anxiety for the future is a dark sun on this Earth,*
*today is burning the atmosphere like greenhouse gas*
*for my people there's no makeup or masks,*
*no Barack Obama to tell them that they can do it.*
*The city that smiles with journalists*
*later says, "Crucify" to too many poor Christs*
*and the present sometimes generates its own dramas,*
*and sometimes gives the mic to a kid of 15.*
*Every day over the Corso celebrates its own gods,*
*every night sings the blues like Lady Day*
*and there's no stadium, no drugs,*
*there's no way out,*
*life runs like blood from this wound.*
*A thousand colors together just make gray,*
*a song comes on the radio that says Losing My Religion,*
*I turn it off, I play what I'm dealt*
*I finish another line, chant down Babylon.*

৵

The moment comes to present the album and clearly it's not an evening like any other. I've been on thousands of stages, but playing in my own town is different. I'm always thrilled but also nervous. We want everything to be perfect.

We meet Filippo Cogliandro, who is one of the most renowned chefs in town. At that time he owns a large banquet hall in Lazzaro, south of Reggio, called the Accademia. His cooking is not the only reason we admire Filippo: He has refused to pay the "protection money" on his business, he's been threatened, he has reported the extortionists and had them arrested. We like each other immediately and decide to present our album in his place. The entrance will be free.

It doesn't seem like a very intelligent choice from a marketing point of view: Just at the moment that all the clubs in town are eager to have us and to pay well, we decide to play for free and to hold the concert in a place that is kilometers away from town, forcing the audience to drive down the 106 Jonica to reach the spot. The Accademia is a restaurant, so there is no stage, nor is there a sound system. We build everything, literally, at the back of the hall. Behind us are some Greek columns, they may be perfect for an elegant wedding, but they're certainly an odd setting for a rap concert. It's the evening of December 26. The restaurant is near the beach, and of course that evening there is a spectacular storm. The waves wash up on the breakwaters, they seem to want to shatter them, enormous splashes of foam rise up. It starts to rain. We finish carrying the sound system, quietly cursing. The room is empty, enormous, dark. There's just the shine of the marble floors, which make it look like a silent and empty church.

This churchlike place, however, slowly fills up incredibly. The view is amazing in every direction. We have prepared a standard show that lasts one hour, and we end up playing for two and a half hours. Filippo, the chef, for once has abandoned his post in the kitchen and is preparing cocktails big and small. He laughs while he shakers the ingredients, he seems to be having a really good time as a barman. The stand where the CDs are on sale is under siege, and so are we. We can physically feel the embrace of the city of Reggio that shares our message, that does not give in to the 'Ndrangheta, and that believes in music as an instrument of resistance. "Everyone came," we say to each other, "Everyone."

≈

The atmosphere in places where struggles are connected to the territory is a different, rarefied one, and here sound seems to travel faster. I notice this when I take my rhymes to the shores of the Strait, to Palestine, to the No Muos base in Niscemi. And then there is the Val di Susa, which no doubt deserves a tale of its own.

The rugby tournament has just ended. The air is clear in the Val di Susa, it's a Sunday, the scene is quite a singular one. One after the other, the balls fly over the fences of the construction site, tracing perfect parabolas, and fall bouncing irregularly, as oval shaped balls do, a few centimeters away from the heavy boots of the riot-control agents, who observe the scene with ill-concealed concern.

On this side of the fences and the barbed wire a line of big men and some ladies compete over who can throw the ball the furthest amid loud laughter and slaps on the back that would crack less-sturdy shoulders.

The previous evening, I performed in the valley, I got up late and missed the morning matches. Fortunately, I get there in time for the most exciting and unusual third half I've ever seen.

It was Lo Zio's idea to end the tournament like this (as a rapper I'm aware that the word *zio*, or *uncle*, should be used as little as possible, but I'm not sure he'd like his name to appear here, and that is what everyone calls him anyway, so I'll stick to it).

Lo Zio is indeed the uncle everyone would like to have: With longish gray hair, he resembles a prophet from the

Bible; he has enormous shoulders, an amused gaze, and some idea or intuition always in mind. He was the one who made the trophies for the winners of the tournament using barbed wire and tear-gas cartridges. He was also the one who organized the haka in front of the construction site that appeared in all Italian media. He recruited me to write the team anthem and thanked me by making me honorary member. I also received a uniform I'm terribly proud of.

*"Hymn Rugby Team No Tav, No Bridge, No Muos (2013)"*

*From Niscemi to the Clarea you go down to the field where I wait for you*
*Here the push of the throng destroys the bridge over the Strait*
*crazy old men and fighters, let's defend our territory*
*from the attack by the Mafia, marines, and speculators*
*my band is penniless, we have functioning hearts and heads*
*I have time and at the after-match dinner I drink with the All Reds in Rome*
*only sea in the Strait, only green in Val di Susa*
*and in Sicily open skies, not colonialism USA*
*you support this team and only if the fight pays*
*voice loud and hands in the air when another haka begins*
*mouthpieces and blockings against blunt bodies:*
*Robocop, Rambo in uniforms are servants of the powerful*
*with the boys and the girls, with the sun and the storm,*
*with the cheer that rises and bounces the oval ball*
*old glories of the neighborhood and the young guys around 20*
*kick hard, throw back, and always run ahead.*

# 2014–2016

The beginning of 2014: I'm asked to take part in Hip-Hop Smash the Wall, a project set up in collaboration with the Palestinian scene and that also involves a trip to the West Bank. At that point, the situation in the occupied territories is one of the calmest in a long time. There is a dialogue between the authorities of the two sides, olive trees are being planted, and there seems to be no sign of the hell that is going to break out in Gaza; or at least we have no clue of what is about to happen.

I already knew something of Palestinian hip-hop, although I was no expert. I was on stage with Shadia Mansour more than once, I know that a nice song by the DAM is called "G'areeb fi blade," which means "foreigner in my nation," and it makes me think of a piece by Sangue Misto that is one of my all-time favorites. The music scene is younger than the Italian one but culturally very advanced: Apart from Arabic they also use English and even Hebrew for their lyrics. From a technical point of view the fast and breathtaking verses like the ones of Busta Rhymes or Tech N9ne are not very popular; and as for the lyrics, there are some political and social messages that remind me of our Assalti Frontali but also some profound lyrical references that echo Middle-Eastern poetry and literature.

At the beginning it seems that the project is little more than a cultural exchange: A group of Italian hip-hoppers flies to the West Bank to collaborate with local counterparts. A rap record, a wall covered in graffiti, some break dance choreography, and finally a live performance and the shooting of a documentary. Eleonora Pochi, who is the project coordinator, reassures us and tells us about the long experience of Assopace in the Palestinian territories. I accept immediately, full of enthusiasm. But, as everyone knows, circumstances change rapidly in the course of only a few weeks, and so it is that we find ourselves flying over Ben Gurion airport in Tel Aviv while the rubble in the West Bank is still smoking, metaphorically speaking.

When going to Palestine the trip begins long before you take off: You must memorize the safety procedures necessary to avoid all kinds of problems when landing in Israel and at the checkpoints. Seen from above, Tel Aviv looks like Miami, but on the ground the feeling of "Western normality" is crushed by policemen wearing bulletproof vests and carrying assault rifles who seem to be on every corner.

The moment we meet the Palestinian part of the team, our three breakers (or b-boys, to be more correct) are the ones who break the ice. Giulia "Chimp," the only b-girl of the group, has lived in these areas and knows the language and the culture (in fact she is the one who works on the documentary for Barbuka Production); then there is Edoardo "Xedo," who jumps in and is the first to start dancing at the center of the circle. The most incredible, however, is Francesco, nicknamed Telemare: After only half an hour he's already the idol of the kids from the Nablus camp, and at the end of the trip he launches into a good-bye speech in Arabic that is full of errors and swear words he's picked up from the rascals.

As for the graffiti (here too a more correct term: writing), when still in Rome, Paolo "Gojo" prepares a huge bag full of bottle caps for the spraycans: They help regulate the quantity and intensity of the spray and are indispensable if you want the best results. In the end caution prevails and

he decides to leave the caps in Rome: It would be too difficult to justify the load on our arrival without disclosing the
artistic and political nature of our trip. The lack of proper
instruments, however, is not always a bad thing: Kids here
usually don't have access to special caps, and in the end
we realize it's more interesting to share and experiment
with the techniques they normally use.

We rappers, as the stereotype says, are initially closed-
off, we need to study one another. Supposedly I'm the militant in the group, but there's also Coez who, with his melodic style, fills concert halls and gets millions of views.
Lucci, though he's part of the same crew as Coez, has a decidedly more hardcore approach: Recall that his last album
is titled *Brutto e Stonato* (Ugly and Out of Tune). Prisma is
perhaps the most meditative, speaking of character, someone who genuinely believes in the values of underground
hip-hop. His crew is called Romanderground. I couldn't
think of a more appropriate name.

The magic doesn't start until we enter the recording
studio, located in a no man's land outside the jurisdiction
of the municipality of Ramallah, on the road to the infa-
mous checkpoint of Kalandia. The moment we pass that
threshold is probably the moment I realize I'm about to
experience something unique, and all the reasons that have
brought us to this corner of the world emerge powerfully.
We start writing and recording as if we've been doing it
together for a lifetime, with the same enthusiasm we used
to use to put pen to paper as kids. Our cameraman Tom
has shown me some scenes he's filmed in the studio, and
the atmosphere is incredible: an impenetrable cloud of
smoke, thousands of empty energy drink cans (they gulp it
down like water), and, in every free corner, an Italian or
Palestinian rapper writing or going over some lyrics, eve-

ryone nodding to their own rhythm. Anyone coming in from outside would think it's an asylum or a meeting of a sect, and in fact those who do stop by to check it out stand immobile, in religious silence.

Chimp explains to me that this studio has a fundamental importance in the history of Palestinian hip-hop: Up until a few years ago, technically one could make professional recordings only within Israeli territory, with enormous economic and logistic difficulties for the local emcees. Khaled, the boy who manages the studio, is a great singer, though he's inexplicably reluctant when it comes to playing his melodies in front of other people. I managed to hear him sing live just once, no recording. At the mixer he's a battle tank: He records, orders sequences, and listens, over and over again. When evening falls he's exhausted, but the work is excellent.

Verse after verse, the album takes shape in a few days. I am the one to break the ice with a song denouncing the occupation and Italy's part in it. Not everyone knows that in the European Union our country is the main provider of weapons and war technology to Israel, with business dealings almost equal to those of Germany, France, and the United Kingdom put together. The album, however, is more than this: We've decided not to focus only on the social aspect, so there's plenty of space for reflective pieces, for talking about feelings and showing off a bit of technique, each in his own language.

"Bringing down the wall" means first of all bringing down the barrier of prejudice, which is another battle hip-hoppers in the region have to fight on the front lines. Rap is not viewed positively by the conservatives, who see it as a medium imported from the United States, for which reason it's automatically labeled as imperialist. In 2007 a concert in Gaza was interrupted abruptly by a group of fundamentalists who beat up four rappers on stage and even kidnapped one for some hours, threatening him with their weapons if he didn't agree to stop playing "corrupt music." As far as I'm concerned, one of the unforgettable scenes, unfortunately, is that of a demonstration by a large group of armed and hooded militiamen directly under the windows of the recording studio. The incursion lasted more than half an hour, with Kalashnikovs firing into the air and children running around collecting cartridges. The police never came, and we finally grasped the real meaning of what was meant when they told us that the studio was in a no man's land.

When we reach the time for the final live performance, we enter the large and beautiful concert hall—the Cultural Palace of Al-Masyoun—pretending we are not the least bit nervous. Italians and Palestinians mix on the huge stage but also among the audience: Our aid workers and the volunteers in the West Bank have gotten the word out, and people have come from Jerusalem, Nablus, Hebron.

The Gaza breakers, on the other hand, have been unable to leave the Strip, although in a certain sense they are with us: Halfway through the show a screen is lowered and an image of them is projected so they can dance virtually with the people who are present. The choreography is extended and perfect, there are no breaks between the traditional music and the driving breakbeat. It's incredible to think that the whole show has been organized in only a few days and with kids who in some cases are only about fifteen.

The performance ends but no one wants to leave the stage. My laptop is already connected to the sound system, the problem is that the only music I have with me is the playlist I made for Michele and Serena's wedding some weeks ago. I find the Run DMC, Lauryn Hill, and then also Kalafro and the Sud Sound System. I press play, look at the screen, and it's another magic moment: Many people from the audience have come on the stage to form a very wide circle for the b-boys. They clap their hands and cheer the most spectacular power moves. The wall dividing the artists from the audience has crumbled spontaneously and we are one.

I notice that I've still got fingers spotted with color: We had spent the day at the graffiti wall, while the people in the area offered fruit and lemonade, and the children asked to have their pictures taken holding the spraycans and posing like painters. Hamza and the other Palestinians wrote *Wattany*, "motherland," filling the black letters with symbols from their tradition. They suggest we write the same thing in Italian, and it starts a discussion among us. The literal translation would be too long, "land" too generic, and "homeland" is out of the question. Finally, we settle on a gigantic "HOME," which Gojo adorns with the symbols of our struggles, from the defence of the territory to the occupied social centers. There is also a hammer and sickle. The experience of Lucci and Coez as writers is equal to their experience with a microphone, and their names take shape on the cement with a style that deserves all the admiration of the locals.

No one is so naive as to think that hip-hop alone will be able to put an end to the Separation Wall or the occupation and the illegal and hateful settlements. But, at these latitudes, there's a revolutionary and progressive movement going, composed of courageous and very intelligent young people. A good enough reason to support their art and struggle.

I've always felt I'm more Mediterranean than European. Geography says that, from Reggio, Ramallah is closer than London. Cultural closeness, however, is more important and precious, and this discovery is the best gift this experience has given me.

*"Hip-hop Smash the Wall (2014)"*

*Stronger than a bomb, deeper than a tomb*
*Music supports the earth and surrounds her*
*Little chatter, I have the sound for combat*
*I'm against the wall and my voice can bring it down*
*The shout goes out strong from Reggio like here in Ramallah,*
*but if I should be afraid I fear only the silent one*
*I loathe prejudice and the ignorance of the racist*
*"Southerner? Mafia," "Palestine? Terrorist."*
*Israel murders, but the bullet is Italian*
*Direct democracy, yes – direct from the money*
*This is why when I sound off you don't feel safe*
*The struggle goes quickly, my voice brings the wall down.*

و

"Un populu diventa poviru e servu quannu ci arrabbanu a lingua" (People become poor and subdued when language is taken from us). The poet Ignazio Buttitta's warning came to mind every time I listened to the songs by Mimmo Martino, and since Martino's death that warning has become all the more urgent and important. Probably not everyone reading this will know who I'm talking about. In this case, you should know that I'm giving you a good piece of advice when I say, listen to him. Mimmo Martino was (is) a unique artist, intellectual, and revolutionary in our South. I'm not going to give you a complete list of his achievements, because others have provided a more authoritative account, and if you want to know more you can easily find information on the web.

The first thing that struck me about him was a move, actually not a very natural one, that he did on stage. He was with Mattanza, his best-known musical group, and was singing "Un Servu e un Cristu" (A Servant and a Christ), a wonderful old hymn to rebellion. When he got to the point when Christ speaks from the cross, Mimmo lifted up the crutch he uses for walking and held it up like a symbol, a weapon, pointing it at the audience. His own cross had become his message and his battle. It hit the people of the audience like a punch in the face, and at the end it seemed the applause would never stop. I was stunned by the power and the simplicity of the message. I wanted to listen to everything he had to say.

The first contacts between us young rappers and this severe father figure were not totally rosy. He acknowledged the immediacy of our communication and the desire to get a message out, but he criticized our superficial approach and our vanity. He basically criticized our use of words such as "roots" and "culture" that we knew little of. Years later, I recognize that he was right.

So, we abandoned the presumptuous idea of sharing the stage with the old maestro (*old* compared to us, who were just kids), but we kept on going to his concerts and listening to his records. We would steal pieces of his songs and sample them to compose our bases. We kept on studying.

In the summer of 2014 I saw Mimmo Martino again after a long time had passed, at the social center Angelina Cartella in Reggio Calabria. It was an evening to raise money to rebuild the only self-managed social space in the city, which was burned down by the usual fascist and mafioso louts. I told him I'd released a rap/blues record with a group of musicians, I wanted him to hear it, but I didn't have the CD with me. So, I sent him a link so he could download it, and that was the end of it. The surprise came some days later, when he wrote to say he liked it a lot and that he wanted a copy. We met again at the Parco del Cartella and spent the evening talking. Forgive me the cliché, but, when he talked about music, Mimmo became a giant. He towered over me, even though I had about ten centimeters and as many kilos on him. He seemed to know my lyrics better than I did and the sound better than my musicians.

The long and short of it was, he told me that it was time to write a song together, and you can imagine how happy I was. Once we'd finished our respective tours and projects, we would surely be in the studio together. But summer 2015 arrived, and we still hadn't been able to write that song together. One evening, when we were about to say goodbye, a mutual friend came up to us, we were talking about our concerts and future plans, which we both had a lot of. He smiled and told us, "Good luck!"

Mimmo Martino, as he was getting up, brandished his crutch, pointed it toward our friend and, also smiling, almost shouted, "And lots of it!"

Six months after his death, I got a phone call from a representative of Mattanza, closing the circle. They wanted me with them on stage at the Teatro Cilea, the most important venue in Reggio, and a place where the most I'd ever done was sit in the audience. The concert was a mix of popular music, rap, poetry, pure electricity. It no longer hurts to remember him and to miss him; the memory has become joy and an awareness of being able to pass on the message and the fight.

At the end of it all, I have the greatest honor and responsibility of repeating the words with which my mentor closed each concert: "A people without history is like a tree without roots: It is destined to die." My parents were there in the audience, smiling and clapping.

*"The Debt (2016)"*

*All the generations of my family are gone.*
*Australia, the U.S., Switzerland, the North*
*"High Italy," as they used to say when I was little.*

*And all the generations of my family have come back, and I am the last.*
*I grew up with the sea and the sun,*
*as all the generations*
*of my family grew up,*
*before leaving.*

*At 18 I left too,*
*like my father, and my grandfather, and their fathers and grandfathers*
*before them.*
*I, I however don't know if I will come back,*
*and honestly the only ones who don't know*
*the faraway blues are those who never experienced it.*

*Sometimes, for an entire week I dream of being home.*
*Literally: for seven nights in a row I close my eyes*
*and my grandmother's there making octopus,*
*and there's a breeze from the veranda*
*and the party feeling in the house*
*from every time I used to return and I return.*

We could be rich, I really think so.
We could make it so that pride
isn't a metal piggybank
with the same little copper pennies
that when you shake it make a sound
and then we feel happy about it.

We could laugh over the fake honor
of fake men of honor
as though it was the red nose of clowns
as though it was a plastic horn.

We could make our land ours
and the money ours and the streets and even public offices and the
     Town Hall
And fatalism – even when it's hot out – could no longer be
neither a wall nor a stone.

We could be no longer a colony,
no longer a suburb
we could defeat the blues
of those who aren't doing well here, and worse when they leave.

We could be young and better.
We could maybe, for once,
pay the debt
of all the generations
who left.

I realize that traveling is another recurring theme in my story, and I also realize that sometimes it isn't necessary to go far in order to travel. Imagine being invited to dinner in the home of strangers. The only thing you know is that they are a family of migrants, but you have no idea of their nationality, of their personal stories, and—although you might not care much—not even what you're going to be served to eat. A small and perhaps inevitable cultural shock, but it's overcome quickly, as soon as you sit down, and at the end of the evening you'll be no doubt grateful for the experience.

This is "Guess Who's Coming to Dinner," one of the most interesting initiatives of the Italian Network of Popular Culture (RICP), an organization I suggest you look up and learn about. It was set up with the aim of preserving and spreading the culture of our territories and its social rites, and in the course of the years it has developed a whole series of events and ideas, among them an excellent free online radio broadcast.

The first time I took part in one of the RICP evenings I found myself on stage improvising together with the poets of *ottava rima*. The challenge between popular poetry and rap was very fun (and I didn't do too bad) but, in all honesty, I must confess that my AABB couplets were much easier to compose than the ABABABCC verses in eight hendecasyllables.

As for the rest, the atmosphere was very similar to what I've seen in many freestyle contests: the style and pride of the participants, the irony and the fun, and a certain electricity that makes no one want to lose and that the audience picks up on and loves.

Today rap is no longer only an imported genre in Italy, and it's time it confronted popular culture the same way it confronts the market and the hit parades every day. Our regions have a rich tradition of rhyme schemes and canons passed on orally, there are still farmers and shepherds who are almost illiterate but who can recite Dante and Tasso (the *ottava rima* was used by Tasso, Ariosto, perhaps first by Boccaccio).

But popular poetry is creation, not only transmission. When I studied Gramsci's theory of the organic intellectual at school, I remember that the first example I thought of was the poets and writers who compose in dialect, workers whose lives were absolutely ordinary but who had a gift of the ability to know and to recount.

You'll pardon my comparison if I say it's up to us rappers (also) to take their place and take the baton. The strong point of our music is (and should be) words and the profound connection with reality and the place we live in. It's not amongst us that the new Supreme Poet must be found, and I'm not asking anyone to learn Tasso's *Gerusalemme Liberata* by heart, but it would be nice — and maybe also possible — to be popular artists who interpret our times with the same strength and credibility of those who came before us.

*"The Bar Blues"*
*(from the album by Kento & the Voodoo Brothers* Radici)

*In the nights when you don't sleep the blues speaks of your memories*
*A thousand beers are a strange lullaby for insomniacs*
*Same bar in those evenings, with the same four drinking*
*I write great truths on the bottom of the coaster*
*Some years earlier I was on the same stool*
*But I was then closer to 20 years than to 40*
*But the more I write in rhymes the more I realize that you don't change*

That I am the same as the first among them the debts and the gray hairs
I have this trace that holds me and encircles me
And she grows more beautiful because she makes herself more womanly
I take a sip and the next, we talk of Che
Of the films of Volonté, of a world that doesn't exist
In the middle of slot machines and video poker for those who haven't
    given up
The cheap dream of the underclass
And I understand that every night there's someone talking
Not to tell tales but not to forget them at dawn.

Down here another warm night like the South
You there, take another swig of rum;
The sound refills these nights, so sit down
And pour yourself another glass.

We're sad and human like train station bars
And the tracks are thoughts and the passengers notes of songs
Passed dreams in the memories of summers
If life brings bitters, coffee in glasses and distilled liquors
And the most different garment is often a distraction
But the darkness is complete so each one is a humble star
Tonight at the bar he tells too many truths
Between those who sing for love and those who curse for necessity
Cops out of uniform to repress crime
But the grass in this war has more soldiers than the army
Throw-up black and silver, cement, vandals, and art
Fights for ten cards, rhythms in up- and downbeat
Thick like crude oil, brief only on the page
Between the phantasms like Kafka but I don't know when to say enough
    to her
The night is a woman and to that degree you must love her
You tell her your stories and she forgets them at dawn.

Once the "Resistenza Sonora" tour with Kalafro is over, the time comes when I feel the need to work on a new record on my own, as Kento. I listen to the previous one again: I still identify with it, I wouldn't change a rhyme, or just about. So, I decide to do something completely different, something that has been done rarely around here: I put together a group of musicians and try to compose a rap album that is completely played and not sampled. What sound am I looking for? I think about it, I listen to the rap records I like from a sound perspective, and the choice is clear to me: It's a time when hip-hop was nervy enough to experiment, to push its boundaries. In the 1990s they'd sample the marvelous funk of the 1970s, and I loved it. In 2000 rappers started to use samples of electronic music of the 1980s, and I liked that a bit less. In the first decade of the new century some even reconsidered and used Eurodance from the 1990s, which I honestly can't stand. So, I tell myself: OK, I want to experiment, but I want to do it my way. I don't want to be chasing something, but to look over my shoulder.

Rap is just one of the youngest branches of the large tree of African-American music: it all comes from spirituals, from early jazz, from the delta blues of the 1920s. This is what the sound of my record will be. And it's also clear to me that the title will be *Radici* (Roots), to reflect this line of thought, but also to pay homage to the Roots, one of the groups that has inspired me the most this way; to remember the record of the same name by Guccini, released in 1972; to highlight my own personal roots: the South, Calabria, my neighborhood. Also, the name we give the group is an ironic homage to the imagery of Louisiana and Mississippi: The Voodoo Brothers, a cauldron of bewitched and boiling sound.

*"Voodoo"*
*(from the album by Kento & the Voodoo Brothers* Radici)

*Tonight the sound is voodoo and blood is trickling down already in the*
 *check*
*Kento microphone warrior, silverback gorilla*
*a revolutionary I come up from the country*
*I bite at the jugular, others bite their tongues*
*I multiply the voice, when I rhyme it's like a chorus*
*And I haven't made a new record; I made something record anew*
*Never a puppet in the hands of the State*
*And my hero is neither a priest nor a judge*
*I'm with the South and its people and its woes*
*And every rhyme I throw at you with is like a hook by Lenny Botai*
*In my curriculum I study the real*
*1,000 books, 1,000 records and something like 100,000 roads*
*say Kento on the poster*
*while too many gold records are paper and plastic*
*I spit on the ground and laugh at this Babylon*
*I play with more rawness, their voodoo doesn't work on me*
*Tonight Voodoo plays, I throw out a darker sound*
*Daggers in my eyes, no one is safe anymore*
*Tonight Voodoo plays, I throw out a darker sound*
*The system that wants us to face the wall will hit harder*
*If the rich guy treats the world as if it was his*
*I support Val di Susa, no bridge, no MUOS.*
*Kento, Voodoo Brothers, Ice One, what do you want to tell us?*
*I drink together with Havoc, I play RC to Queensbridge.*
*This is Voodoo like the blues in Louisiana*
*I run like the Mississippi among the troubles of this bitter life*

*And if hip-hop today is soft and is clean*
*I'm dirty, old wood, rusty metal*
*chicken blood on the fetishes of this society*
*always with more "reality" and always less reality*
*This is the bullet of the revolution*
*Caught in the exact moment at which it hits the dictator*
*Because of that, I'm not in line at the fashion places*
*But drinking beer behind the stage at the concert*
*I bring revolt to the street and to the scene*
*Every independent mind breaks up the voodoo of the system.*

There are two questions that I get asked more than others: the first is can rappers be considered as today's singer-songwriters; and the second one is can rap be considered poetry.

These are actually two difficult questions, to which there might not be an answer. The singer-songwriters in the 1960s and 1970s might be similar to us in that they felt the need to narrate the reality unfolding in front of them, the changes, the protest movements of the young. What is different is the sound, the beat, in part the inspiration. Overall, what is different is the social impact they created with their songs. The history of Italian music — and perhaps also Italian history in general — would be very different without our Guccini, Fabrizio De André, Paolo Pietrangeli, Claudio Lolli. And from this perspective, honestly, we can still look at them only through a pair of binoculars. Claims to the contrary, as far as I can see, are meaningless, or they are aimed at promoting a single rapper who is labeled the "heir of."

I meet Paolo Pietrangeli at one of his concerts, in a tiny and crowded club. He sings them all, from the legendary *Contessa* to the newer tracks, like the beautiful "Fiore di

Gaza." At the end of the evening I see him standing in a corner outside, smoking his pipe. I pluck up my courage and tell him I play music and that it would be an honor to collaborate with him. "What kind?" he asks. "Rap," I answer, obviously, and it seems to me that he gives me a perplexed look. I manage to get a "We'll talk about it" out of him, before he disappears behind a cloud of smoke.

I discover that we are neighbors, and I set off by foot to go and pay him a visit. The maps, however, don't tell me that from the entrance there is another kilometer to walk uphill, and when I get there I have to pause to catch my breath. Pietrangeli takes everything very seriously, as it should be. He asks to listen to the music and then wants to read the lyrics. We have a discussion regarding my use of the term "mass," he wants to know if I use it in a Marxist way. We go to the recording studio together: He has written a talking blues; it's poignant, stunning, sharp. He tries a couple of takes to warm up and asks me "How'd they sound?" and I have the surreal experience of giving feedback to an Italian music legend.

*"Hazet 36"*
*(from the album by Kento & the Voodoo Brothers* Radici)

*I still am looking for a word to sing it*
*between pages of books or balanced on my pentagram*
*I want the blood to run in between its letters*
*a mosaic without a composition, a simple transmission*
*that doesn't make miracles but shines light in the corners*
*like certain records by Guccini and by Pietrangeli*
*story-singer more than storyteller*
*but if music is unique, hand me the proof*
*sentences in notebooks already are burning up minds*

*they're building universes with voices and instruments*
*repression has continued since the times of Valle Giulia*
*but my people don't flee, they're stronger than fear*
*and our black ink makes dust of the gunshot*
*all that's left is to resist; it's a new Stalingrad*
*and if the enemy is still the one from those years*
*we've already beaten him and now we have new weapons.*

*I know that without music tomorrow will be worse*
*silence turns air to ice even in August in Reggio*
*the lead of the '70s today is white powder*
*who is the slave down in Rosarno and who is the slave of a bank*
*raise the volume of the earnings or of the guitar*
*it won't reach the masses if the singer doesn't speak about it*
*antagonist to every fake alternative*
*my microphone is the Hazet 36 of the third millennium*
*this is why I put the words in a stereo*
*and I have the torment of a poet but without the genius*
*I play louder than plastic and Kalashnikov*
*the kids in the piazza and some old anarchists listen to me*
*anti-state, but I have the memory of the past*
*and I know that freedom doesn't exist in the free market*
*and I speak clearly because what's in me is clear*
*I am always moving, the revolution is the wind.*

I call the best musicians I know. Surprisingly they all accept: We start to work on the album. I learn, at my own expense, that it's much more difficult than writing over beats: the first times in the recording studio I honestly have no idea what I'm doing, the boys are asking "do you prefer this variation or this one?" and I can't tell the difference. It is a healthy exercise in humility at a moment when I was feeling I had it all and at the same time a warning that the musical creative process is much more complex than what I was used to. The creation of *Radici* took almost three years: choosing musicians of such high caliber meant running the risk of their going on tour for three months to work on a solo project, and putting them all together to work is a crap shoot. The positive side is that experiences build up in real time and enrich the project, while the sound has the chance to settle and gradually become full-bodied, like a fine wine.

*Radici* is released in 2014, and it's very well received: At the end of the year it's among the top ten in journalists' and industry charts, but what surprises me the most is to see it finish, in a thematic classification, as one of the year's three best blues records. The journalist who wrote about it is considered to be an authority in this field, and because up until recently I would never have dreamed of considering myself a bluesman, I'm terribly proud of such a recognition.

✌

In the meantime, I embark on a journey that will decisively influence my writing and my vision of hip-hop: a series of workshops in some juvenile-detention centers. A activist friend of mine organizes everything and also takes care of the paper work (which, in these cases, is not a small task), and I find myself crossing the threshold of various youth detention centers in several cities. I am tasked with respecting the privacy of these kids and I don't want to create problems for the organizations that allowed me to have this experience, so you'll understand that I'm not being reticent if I omit some details, such as the names of the cities and of the detention centers. It's good to remember that, not being myself an expert on education, during these lessons/workshops, I was always with a specialist or by a teacher.

The feeling of standing in front of the entrance of a juvenile detention center is not a nice one. The door is always heavy and oppressive, the security procedures always strict. When entering you are carefully instructed to leave behind not only your telephone and other communication devices, but also potentially blunt objects such as keys and even pens. Christmas is approaching, and we have brought a couple of cakes and plastic knives to cut them. The guard at the door is unyielding: The cakes must be sliced before entering and the knives must be left outside. The director of one of the structures explains to me that the problem is not only fights, but also self-harm: One of the boys managed to break a neon tube and eat some pieces of it in order to not be transferred to the jail for adults when he turned eighteen. Others, for the same reason, have sewn their mouth and eyes with makeshift needles. There are even cases of genital self-injury and, unfortunately, riots between different ethnic groups.

Following these preliminaries, meeting the boys is a pleasant surprise. The arrival of someone who does music is always an event for them; also, at that age, they all listen to rap and almost all of them compose rhymes or do breakdance. At the beginning it's always up to me to break the ice, so I start rapping. At that point it's automatic that someone becomes enthusiastic, and if I'm clever enough to keep the enthusiasm going, we're up and running. We start to exchange rhymes like in any of the circles that form at the corner of streets or outside clubs. Each boy wants to demonstrate his ability, his style, his way of telling reality.

Usually a couple of boys have been to jams, and they are the most professional: perfectly in time, battle-ready rhymes, they could be on stage. Then there is always the boy who doesn't miss a word but remains on the sidelines, and if you manage to convince him he'll deliver the most moving verses.

I'm stopped by a boy from Eastern Europe. The face of an adult, he acts tough, a tattooed "Thug Life." He's written a song called "Mi Chiedo (I ask myself)," and I tell him I'd like to hear it. He delivers three minutes of pure poetry: He asks about his future, he asks does life end at sixteen, he asks why is he starting to reflect on life only now that he's in jail. I lean against the wall, literally speechless.

Another boy, from North Africa, has a clear psychological issue. He almost looks like a child. He says: "I've written one hundred songs!" and I obviously answer that I want to hear them all. The "songs" all start in the same way, with him being summoned by the director of the jail. But they all have a different ending: In one he is freed, in another he is punished, in another one his mother—he hasn't seen her in years—is waiting for him in the director's office. Here too I am amazed by the expressive power and the liberating charge.

Still another, with the attitude of a seasoned veteran, tells me he wants to make it big as a rapper, be respected by everyone, get girls, and, especially, make a ton of money so he won't have to steal any more. I encourage him, I tell him to work hard, that history is full of rappers who wrote their most successful albums in a prison cell. Honestly I don't know if he'll make a ton of money, but I'm sure that writing, believing in yourself, and pursuing a dream will make him grow and make him feel better.

In the end, I try to conclude without getting too heavy on them and say just: "Respect yourselves, respect your fellow prisoners, and be brave." There's a lot more I'd like to add. In my experience, each and every one of them has been nothing but fraternal toward me. I haven't met any criminal, nor have I met anyone who "chose the wrong path in life," but only kids who, if they'd had a family or decent economic means, or even just a roof to sleep under or a good lawyer to represent them, wouldn't be behind those bars. The offences they've committed are typically two: petty theft and mild drug pushing. The social groups are the most marginalized ones: foreigners, children of immigrants, Roma people. The only thing these kids are guilty of is being poor, in all the possible meanings of the word. These kids are victims of the judiciary system's most inhumane side and, in the last analysis, of capitalism.

These are, literally, the words I use during an interview: The workshop experience is going to be the subject of a documentary, filming is still taking place, inside and outside the jail. I must emphasize that I only encourage the boys, I don't try to fill their heads with crazy ideas, but in this moment the jail is a faraway place, and when I'm asked a direct question I can only give a clear answer. After all, what's the sense of being a rapper if I can't tell things as they are?

Sometime later, the association that runs the project informs me that there have been some problems with the director of a facility. It seems that my words have not been well received, and I'm asked to take back what I've said. I can't: I tell them I prefer to be taken out of the documentary rather than say things I don't believe. The other activists involved in the project are on my side and say they are also ready to call the whole thing off. The discussion escalates. The project for the hip-hop workshops is suddenly interrupted, and the association receives an injunction in which it is stated that the authorization for filming was never granted... But how is this possible? The plastic knife to cut the cake was confiscated, but a whole crew, equipped with cameras and even a boom microphone, was let in without permission?

The ones affected the most, as always, are the weak ones: the young inmates, who lose the weekly appointment they look forward to so much, for no reason. Thinking back on it, I don't think I made the right decision. I chose to be consistent, which cost me nothing, while I could have been a bit more accommodating and continue an experience that was indeed very significant.

❧

Just when I'm immersed in these reflections, I get a phone call, totally unexpected, in which I'm told that *Radici* has won the "Culture Against the Mafia" prize. I know that the jury member who backed me with the strongest conviction is Stefano Cuzzocrea, a friend and music journalist of great culture (not to mention his past as an old-school Calabrian rapper!). I call him, thank him, we go out to lunch together. Stefano is in a good mood: Skinny as he is, he eats a rare cooked steak bigger than the plate. He insists on paying, he tells me it's a good day, he's just undergone difficult surgery. I share an anecdote with him: Some years earlier, he'd organized a screening of a film, *Rockers*, a critical movie for understanding the Jamaican reggae scene of the 1970s. Obviously, I went. Not many people came to the show and Stefano came up to me, almost as if to apologize, but I was in seventh heaven: I'd taken advantage of such a specific and interesting film to show off with a girl I was dating. We ended up together, so what my friend remembered as a flop for me was the beginning of something terrific. From that moment, every time Stefano saw me with Camilla, he always made fun of me, and recalled that evening in a small club in the Testaccio neighborhood.

My smile becomes painful if I think of how that day, in front of a steak, was the last time I saw him so cheerful. His illness got the better of him, though he lives on in our memories, in his writings, in the recollection of that dark room where, on screen, Horsemouth rides his motorbike to take his records to the all the sound systems in Kingston.

ळ

I go to Faenza to accept the "Culture Against the Mafia" award at the beginning of October 2014. I have the feeling I can't get my bearings. I still have Palestine in my eyes, because I just got back from there, and I had a live performance the night before, so I've slept maybe three hours. The stage is one of the most important ones in the Italian scene: the Meeting of the Independent Labels. The representatives of the DaSud Association award me the prize.

DaSud is one the most wonderful organizations I know: Their headquarters are in Rome, but the group is made up mostly of Southerners like myself, it's been fighting the Mafia for ten years already, a fight they wage with seriousness and rigor, but also with imagination and a smile. Composed of journalists and researchers, but also artists, students, and people with all types of backgrounds, it has launched some of the most important campaigns in recent years, aimed at making known and examining the Mafia phenomenon in all its forms, not least the latest one, which is known in the press as Mafia Capitale.

I've known Danilo and Pasquale, who present me the prize, from before we started shaving, and backstage the conversation turns in no time to planning. "What about working on an album together, Kento and DaSud?" "Let's talk about it!" I realize another spark has struck, and it's only a matter of time before it turns into a fire.

We all head back to Rome, we see each other again, and the project gets going: DaSud immediately gives me a series of beautiful prompts and the inspiration for composing my next album. I talk to the boys in the band, and they also get on board: We officially start working on the next Kento & The Voodoo Brothers album: It will be called *DaSud*.

"I Come from the South"
(from the album by Kento & the Voodoo Brothers Da Sud)

*The fighter's heart is a wild beast*
*It's held prisoner in the thoracic cage*
*A closed fist against the sky, a tear on the cheek*
*I come from the South, I tell you: I come from the South.*

*It's not a return; I never went away*
*The same face, same struggles, same barricades*
*Same hatred of fascism and the middle class*
*Kento flows on like the blood in the streets*
*I come from the South like the Mafia and dialect*
*You hear the accent in every syllable I say*
*I am a son of brigands, a cursed one*
*Jesus loves me; I see him more like a friend*

*And fake gangsters wage a fake war*
*Up for grabs is rank and two grams of mannitol*
*The real Mafia meanwhile is murdering my land*
*You rappers really don't know what you're talking about*
*And I already said it: my voice is like a chorus*
*I am the South that today is scattered all over Italy*
*So, when I rhyme I'm never alone*
*On the stage we are a hundred million.*

*I wrote a verse for every one of the fallen comrades*
*And I know that heaven probably doesn't exist*
*For Valarioti and Nistico, for all our ranks*
*The only eternity is in the fist of the one who resists*
*The mind of the one who struggles is a wild beast*
*Filled with love as much as it seems hostile*
*A tightly held prisoner in the cranial box*
*Only the one who hears that she's pushing can understand it*
*And I never thought that of us Southerners*
*Today it could be said that we do not remember:*
*But how can you say "Italy for Italians"*
*If your father was subjected to racism in the first person?*
*Tonight I am writing, the wine stains my page*
*But it's OK, it seems to bring good luck*
*Every other city is to the South of another*
*Except if you live at the North Pole or on the moon.*

It's been said many times that the South is a place of the mind, and I think so too. In order to write this new album I immerse myself in a series of new readings and go back to texts I studied a few years ago, from Amiri Baraka to Angela Davis, Saverio Strati and Gianni Rodari. I have ten dense and powerful pieces in mind that tell the strongest stories I've ever told. The sound, also, is promising: The

Voodoo Brothers are an experienced crew, and this time we also have the chance to use the marvelous recording studios of the Casa del Jazz, an opportunity we seize immediately.

I've been wanting to write a song about Totò Speranza for a long time, and I finally put pen to paper and the lyrics come to life. The story of Totò tells a lot about my land: He was the bass player for a historic reggae group from Calabria, called Invece, and was killed by the 'Ndrangheta in March 1997 for a small marijuana debt of 300,000 lire. His story understandably touched everyone who made music and hated the 'Ndrangheta. The two verses practically compose themselves, and it seems like the obvious choice to call Nicola of Kalafro to write the refrain, to close the circle we opened some years ago with *Resistenza Sonora*.

"*Totò Speranza*"
(*from the album by Kento & the Voodoo Brothers* Da Sud)

*My name is Totò and I play the bass in a band*
*28 years, big dreams like mine because*
*all around a blue ocean as far as the eye can see*
*and the waves are like the hypnotic reggae loop*
*we are the Instead, a great group and a great name*
*many people listen to us at parties and at the occupation*
*I'm no saint: I've done my stupid shit*
*but a man with no faults is not a man, what you going to do?*
*March in Bovalino seems already like spring*
*the wind blows softly like it softly becomes evening*
*and a real life is better than a serious life*
*and some people have never lived in a complete life*
*I roll one and then I light it and smile*
*the smoke fills the air and it's my last breath*

*a silence falls and the darkness fills the room*
*tonight the dream of Totò Speranza is told.*

*From up here I look out at you and, fuck, you all look the same*
*lost in your own problems and mental schemes*
*behind that system that still enslaves you*
*human beings, learn to be human beings*
*my brother, rebel; my sister, fight*
*to love this land of ours means loving you*
*while you grow old I will stay young forever*
*Totò who stares at the ocean with the eyes of a 28-year-old*
*with a lit joint and the air of one who challenges the world*
*and if you ask me what I want, I smile and don't answer*
*look in the mirror, we are the same person*
*we are both on the same end of the gun*
*and my power is the love that conquers us*
*and my music the touch of every bassist*
*rips the silence, now the sound fills the room*
*tonight the dream of Totò Speranza is told.*

There are many stories that deserve to be told, too many to be told in one career, let alone in one album with ten songs. Cinzia, a member of DaSud, tells me the story of Denise Cosco: her mother, Lea Garofalo, was savagely killed and burnt because she collaborated with the judges who were fighting the 'Ndrangheta, and Denise had the courage to turn her own father in. It's a terrible story, but it's also a story about how it is possible to rebel against a destiny that many believe is encoded in the family's DNA, so it's also a story of liberation and hope. I've never met Denise, I've never even seen her: She is hiding under witness protection. In the song I can only imagine a meeting that has never actually taken place.

*"Denise"*
*(from the album by Kento & the Voodoo Brothers **Da Sud**)*

*Denise is looking at me, she smiles only with her eyes*
*she says that she sees the dawn after too many years of nights*
*the lights this morning are like broken fragments*
*she turns around calmly, almost transparent amidst the blocks.*
*All around is the traffic, and it's music in delay*
*and mirrors of the puddles that don't know who you are*
*so I repeat: I wouldn't have had her courage*
*but I try to keep my back straight, like her.*
*Imagine if you lost everything, like confronting grief*
*take your dry heart and make it become a fruit.*
*Bitter days, when you would like to rest*
*But love doesn't want someone with no love to give.*
*If it were up to her, Denise would look forward*
*she wouldn't want to be older than her years.*
*The wind's died down, maybe today the weather will improve ...*
*If it were up to her, Denise would still love.*

*Denise doesn't believe that the world revolves around her*
*she keeps walking and the dawn appears every day*
*some people trade love for pride*
*as though they themselves didn't need it*
*and at 20 years old everyone wants to escape*
*but Denise is different, among the people at the funeral*
*despite the wounds she dreams of a normal life*
*in the embrace of the piazza that makes a cathedral for her*
*as much as I can find the words*
*If there's no life in them they can't walk alone*
*And it isn't what you write but what you do that speaks*
*Denise I can't live her but I can speak of her.*

*She doesn't find space in the TG in the middle of the evening*
*And in the deafening normalcy of a young warrior*
*Denise doesn't want people to call her an example*
*and in the end even this is a step toward change.*

*So, smile, defeat fear*
*You who are change will walk safely*
*The road is hard and we are born without wings*
*But your road is the only one that will lead to tomorrow.*

❧

There are so many topics to cover, and to introduce my next reflection I have to take a step back. Hip-hop is not a neutral culture. It was born in the African-American neighborhoods, by definition it rejects racism, and since day one it has conveyed the message of personal and social liberation. Probably its political nature ends here, because over the years it has been used for expressing the most diverse and conflicting ideas, becoming also, in some instances, superficial and hedonistic, and even an icon of stars-and-stripes consumerism. Hip-hop doesn't necessarily mean shouting "fight the power," like Public Enemy; however, this does not mean that our community doesn't set boundaries that shouldn't be overstepped.

Now, it's not true that Italian rap risks becoming racist, and I won't be the one to launch this false alarm. Italian rap, however, risks becoming indifferent, and this is equally unacceptable. I started thinking about this because of the events that took place at the beginning of 2015, when some underground artists (including myself of course) became supporters of the #MaiConSalvini[7] movement and took part in the antiracist and antifascist demonstration held in Rome on Saturday, February 28. Because of this stand some rappers were unexpectedly subjected to insults and threats.

The same happened after the No Expo demonstration[8] on May 1, 2015, in Milan, when I made the *mistake* of publishing, on my artist's page on Facebook, the photo of a policeman launching tear gas at eye level, claiming that if the tear gas had hit someone in the face the person would have suffered serious injuries. When I (literally) reached two hundred comments saying things like "too bad it was only teargas and not buckshot," or "they should kill them all," along with comments saying I should stick to playing music and abstain from comments like these, I got tired of it and deleted the photo. It's obviously one of those stupid things that happen on social media, but it makes me stop and think: how many covert Nazis follow my politically partisan page? Also, if this happens on Kento's page, what happens on the pages of more famous or less politicized artists?

On the other hand, we have Casapound[9] and the extreme right trying to intercept youth cultures, and after having covered the city with grotesque posters in which they try to appropriate Rino Gaetano and Che Guevara, now they are attempting to organize hip-hop concerts (which are, to be honest, just as grotesque) and graffiti conventions (this is the most ridiculous thing of all, seeing

---

[7] Matteo Salvini, the leader of the rightest Lega party (Trans.).

[8] Protests by immigrant-rights and workers representatives held in Milan against them Prime Minister Matteo Renzi's Milan Expo (Trans.).

[9] Fascist off-shoot movement named after Ezra Pound (Trans).

as only yesterday the fascists were the guardians of order with their punitive campaigns against writers).

From my point of view, what is happening is simple: Rap has become a mainstream genre that more or less all kids listen to, including kids that are stupid or confused enough to identify with fascism or racism and to join groups that support this rubbish. Why doesn't the music scene take a unanimous stand? Why are there only a few rappers who are openly antifascist and antiracist? Maybe I'm the one who is distrustful, but I strongly suspect that in some cases rappers fear that if they expose themselves they will lose fans, views on YouTube, copies sold, and so on.

In a different context, the hip-hop scene in the U.S. almost unanimously sided with Occupy Wall Street, and rappers continued to sell records and hold concerts without any problems. In fact, this experience made them stronger and more authoritative, because they proved they were able to play a positive and important role in the progress of society.

Now the request I'd like to explicitly address to the whole Italian hip-hop scene is to choose to reject fascism and racism of every kind. We have to say that we don't want fascists and racists at our concerts or on our Facebook pages. On our records we can speak of revolution — like I do — the same way we talk about weed and girls, but we mustn't give our enemies the chance, not even accidentally, to infiltrate our culture. It's something I've already talked about and I will go on talking about it until we reach this minimum degree of social collective awareness as a movement.

"Piazzale Loreto"
(from the album by Kento & the Voodoo Brothers **Da Sud**)

I see the fascists of yesterday and today, with jacket and tie and brief-
case
Bringing the money that serves to pay the Mafia with corruption
It's called Mafia Capital, it is that electoral system
In which the comrade serves because it makes a servant of money
And in the meetings, they increase hatred, they stick to their guns like a
good soldier
They despise the gypsies, but they certainly don't hate the money that
they brought them
And a false left collects and ignores it
but don't call yourself antifascist if you do business with this people
bring the money, they book the band, bring the Celtic cross to the Ger-
man throat
I bring fire and gas in every rhyme of mine and I know that they will
burn
Only hatred for CasaPound, Alba Dorata, and their slogans
And for those who have taken old shit and called it Forza Nuova
Up until yesterday they were the guardians of clean walls and decorum
Now they have conventions for rap and graffiti so people will talk about
them
This is why I bring resistance, not a step back
Every stage I step on is the Piazzale Loreto.

And to say that fascism doesn't exist anymore is the excuse of the indif-
ferent
It's washed its face, put on a jacket, and stayed the same shit as ever
I know that Dax resists still and hates those who murder him
Every day, in silence, in the name of his quiet living
I am with the same comrades as always who have kept my back
At school and in the square, rap is a farce, I refute this fucking scene

*How is it that some topics only get talked about by Kento*
*Whereas you don't say anything, like you've dropped the mic*
*I saw them in social centers posing like militant mc's*
*Who would kiss Salvini's ass if they had money in front of them*
*We are the defeated who will take over tomorrow*
*We are rich, yes, in everything except material goods*
*As long as I have a rhyme, blood, and saliva, a pen on paper and satire*
*As long as the struggle makes the difference, my resistance continues*
*This evening this place is ours, we're not giving up an inch*
*Every stage I step on is Piazzale Loreto.*

*I remain antifascist – Piazzale Loreto*
*The end of the racist is in Piazzale Loreto*
*To change your view you have to keep your head down*
*You don't like my music? It doesn't like you.*

# Today and Tomorrow

Between right and wrong choices, good and bad adventures, music is a traveling companion that never abandons me. For a large part of my career (I hate to use the word *career* when talking about music, let's say "for the better part of my artistic journey"), rap has been a niche genre, underestimated, even made fun of. Up to the point when Eminem emerged in the collective consciousness, we were often considered by public opinion just as a bunch of fools wearing loose trousers, gesturing like monkeys making the sign of the horns. So, it's clear that those who started to write rhymes didn't do it to earn any type of consensus, and certainly didn't have any economic ambition. Growing up artistically in an environment of this kind had its benefits, on one hand, especially in small towns you had to have strong will power to get into this culture, and you quickly got used to "keeping it real" (this precept is considered the first rule of hip-hop culture). Personally, it's a liberation: I come from nowhere, I don't expect anything, and I'm ready to go back to the nowhere I come from, if and when rap is forgotten. But let me say: For five or six years now I've been hearing know-it-alls claiming that rap is over and that next year will be the year of the new X genre. Then the X genre comes and fades, and rap is still here.

Notwithstanding all this, I have to take the reflection a little further. I can't deny that the success and the social impact of rap have positively influenced my activity. Ten years ago I was happy to hold one concert a month; now I do fifty or sixty a year (also, the money is decidedly better). I have a group of fantastic musicians; when I want to, I write for one of the most important Italian newspapers; I have labels producing my records, designers giving me clothes; I'm even paid to travel and have incredible experiences with poets and intellectuals whose work just yesterday I would have only read sitting in my room. Nonetheless, I assure you that, even though I've studied and improved, I'm still the same idiot I was ten years ago. What has changed is rap. Or better: Its social role has changed. In part this is because of artists who produce music with content that is, in my opinion, questionable, but who have been able to reach a large public. It's a small paradox: My music is antagonistic and non-aligned, but somehow I too end up enjoying the benefits of the huge growth of the rap audience that's been created by the wave of commercial music.

From a certain point of view, I'm happy that I'm getting such acknowledgement only now, when I'm closer to my forties than to my twenties. It's taken me a long time to work my way up the ladder, and during this period I have also learned to "keep it real," and I think I can say that I know what real life is. Probably as I kid I too would have been overwhelmed by the more frivolous elements of this life, which is what I see happening to some very young rappers who nowadays become stars in a couple of weeks. The main difference, the thing I acquired while I was still rising through the ranks, is that I come from "nothing" so having to go back there wouldn't cause any trauma.

"The Truth"
(from the album Sacco or Vanzetti)

It isn't in the governments or in the parliaments, it doesn't sit at the
    table together with the powerful
It's not in the accounts of any bank, they never saw it at the White
    House.
No surgeon has ever asked it an opinion while getting rid of Silvio's
    wrinkles
It's not in the circles of Forza Nuova nor in the folders of Lele Mora.
It's not in the usual "good mornings" of those hiding their own loneli-
    ness
It doesn't deliver elegies at any funeral, it's not in the not saying any-
    thing so as to cause no harm.
It's not in the silence nor in the too many arguments, not in the every-
    where nor in the hidden places
It's not a giant it's not a butterfly it's not where they tell you you will
    find it.

REFRAIN
It's not in the news broadcasts on TV
It's not on the front page of the newspapers
It's in the silent hospital wards
It shouts an awful lot in family arguments
It's not in the news broadcasts on TV
It's not on the front page of the newspapers
It's with the ones who don't read tomorrow in their palms
It knows how to be a weapon for the same hands.

I hear it in the song of revolution, in every revolt that buries the boss
I see it smiling in the face of death singing that the wind is blowing
    stronger

*I saw it weeping for Carlo Giuliani, shooting in the mountains with the*
*partisans*
*I saw it shine on unknown faces and braid itself into the hair of devoted*
*Rastafarians*
*The Church of Rome has forgotten it, I saw it ignored a million times.*
*Sometimes it discloses and sometimes it promises, and sometimes it is*
*in rhyme in the heads of rappers*
*I saw it weeping, black with anger, in the eyes of the unemployed in*
*Calabria*
*And it is in history, but it lives in the present, it's the only treasure*
*that is ours forever.*

Every now and then, by phone or via the internet, I get a special message that makes me feel proud. It comes from a friend or a stranger, from a city I've visited, or one I've never been to. The important thing is the content: "We're at the march, and they're playing your music."

I remember going to my first marches, where we used to end up almost fighting over the music to play, it was that important to us. I wonder how many words of mine actually reach the kids in all that chaos, in the midst even of police charges and repression. I imagine the sound expanding horizontally in the public squares, rising up in the streets, climbing up the sides of buildings, coming in through the windows. These are the moments I feel sure that what I do has meaning.

Until recently, I would have sworn I remembered all my concerts, one by one. Now that the years have gone by and I can count the live performances in hundreds, this is something I can no longer say, and I'm kind of sorry about that. To write these reminiscences I've tried to bring some order, to put together the pieces of an overall picture so as to preserve the bright colors of each one of the pieces.

Well, I'm not old enough, nor important enough, to write an autobiography, and more than once I've asked myself whether this book might give the impression of being too self-referential, or, simply, seem like a collection of episodes that are merely put together, without a meaningful unifying thread. For sure I've gotten something wrong, mistaken some face or date, gotten things confused. Despite the reassurances of my editor, these doubts remain. But I know there is a meaning, an overall picture that can be grasped.

Music, just like all of the most important contemporary means of expression, comes from the roots. The market may well appropriate a social phenomenon such as hip-hop, but this doesn't change the fact that it was born from a group of urban sub-proletariat residents of the worst neighborhoods in New York. Art belongs to the people not only as a right of enjoyment and of culture, but also from the point of view of primordial creation. We've seen this debate explode in the area of visual art in recent years, with reference to so-called "street art," in terms that we could also relate to rap, almost in the same terms. Having established this, we can say that searching for creative prompts and inspirations in the underground scene is not indicative of a snobbish attitude toward forms of expression that we perceive as "corrupt," or a celebration of the golden age of the 1990s, when rap was still considered pure (there's much more to say about this too). No: Just looking to the street simply means looking to the only place where creativity is still authentic, where the seeds are growing that will infiltrate mainstream music in a couple of years.

Personally, I believe that the best is yet to come. If I thought that hip-hop had died with Tupac, I'd be curled up at home listening to Tupac's records over and over again (Hey! It's something I actually do!), instead of traveling thousands of kilometers every year, using every means of transport to spread my rhymes. I'm sorry Sangue Misto and Lou X aren't making albums anymore, but I'm sure that somewhere, in a basement, a group of kids who are potentially as good are working hard to come and get what they deserve. The fact that today somebody who starts rapping has the possibility of accessing thousands of artists thanks to the web, albums, and videos of live concerts, is a marvelous possibility, one that enables them to make progress very quickly, unlike me: At their age I was memorizing fanzines and sleeping in train stations after seeing this or that concert. The point is that one experience doesn't replace the other. Hip-hop can be told by books, films, records, but it can't be really experienced except in person. As soon as you've finished this book, if I've made you curious, look for an event in your city. Don't look for big names, look for a local artist; it could be a emcee, a dj, b-boy/b-girl, or a writer. Listen and watch without prejudice, try and understand where the artist's inspiration comes from, what he or she is trying to tell you with the performance. If you have the chance, go and talk to someone who represents the scene in your city or in the place closest to where you live. The idea that hip-hop can be found only in large cities is outdated: Some small cities in the country stand out, and others are distinguishing themselves for the originality and depth of their artistic expression.

Clearly not everyone has to be a rapper or a hip-hopper, but probably everyone should have the basic instruments to understand this culture (or counterculture, or subculture, I'm not here to offer definitions) that has become the common language of the young over almost the entire world.

The stupid prejudice of "they're all morons" or "look how they dress" is not very different from what previous generations had to go through at the time of hippies, punks, all the so-called "alternative" cultures. As is the case with all the movements that came before us, there is certainly a degree of affectation and posing, but there is also something profound and interesting that will leave a mark even on people who try to ignore or ridicule hip-hop. Yesterday the kids wearing baggy clothes were aliens; today everyone goes around with a New Era snapback with a flat brim. If twenty years ago someone had told me that an Italian rapper would have won the Sanremo Music Festival and been received by the pope, I would have laughed. To be honest I still feel like laughing, but it's a fact I have to, we all have to, take as a sign of a changing world.

# APPENDICE
## Songs in Italian

### "RC Confidential" (from the album by Kento & The Voodoo Brothers "Radici")

Stanotte è calma, e questa sabbia è ancora calda
E il sorriso lo intuisco e non arriva sulle labbra
Tira i pensieri come reti sulla spiaggia
È un vecchio gioco a perdere, è febbre che mi contagia
E' il miele amaro della nostalgia più intensa
Nel buio anche più immensa, RC Confidential
Perché se piove, l'acqua evapora e scompare
Il sangue è denso e resta il segno sulle strade settimane
Ripenso agli urli nel quartiere e alle bandiere
Alla costanza dei compagni e all'arroganza del potere
Biancheria stesa, le donne velate in chiesa
E i miei disegni sui quaderni per i conti della spesa
I briganti e l'Aspromonte, il mare e l'Isola di fronte
Ed ancora sulla carta la minaccia di quel ponte
Oggi il futuro è già presente e non so più
Se sorridere o deprimermi o descriverlo in un blues.

Mescola accordi e stonature, rumore e silenzio fitto
La città ha mille segreti, compreso il suo stesso ritmo
Quando mi parla devo raccontarla
E il silenzio non è d'oro, chiedi a loro quanto taglia
A chi ha il sole a righe in carcere, a chi muore per rinascere
A chi ha le manette al polso, chiedi al corso, a santi e
    maschere
All'oro al collo, al ferro in tasca, a chi ritorna
A chi dorme in una fossa e a chi sogna California
E ritornelli antichi vivono in nuove ferite
tra il ricordo nelle storie e l'odore della cordite
Censura sull'articolo, dice "non c'è pericolo"
Ma io strappo il giornale, io non credo a ciò che dicono
Per questo non mi importa dei tuoi soldi: sono falsi

O di essere il migliore che il mercato può comprarsi
Io resto con gli stessi in piazza e pochi euro in tasca
Questo posto è troppo grande, questo posto non mi basta
E non resta che scriverle, viverle, mentre le parole uccidono
Amarle e farle nostre, forse oltre ciò che dicono
Tenerle calde in mano e strette come un'arma
Perché in fondo è ciò che sono, ed il suono è vita che parla
E non resta che scriverle, viverle, mentre le parole uccidono
Amarle e farle nostre, forse oltre ciò che dicono
Tenerle calde in mano e strette come un'arma
Perché in fondo è ciò che sono, il mio suono, Reggio Calabria.

**"All'Orizzonte" (from the album "Sacco o Vanzetti")**
Nato in Calabria, seconda metà dei '70
Una famiglia che lottava a far quadrare il conto in banca
E imparo appena a parlare per salutare
Emigriamo prima della prima elementare
E prima spiagge e gabbiani, vento e risacca
E poi il rumore delle fabbriche e la pioggia sulla giacca
A cinque anni o forse meno e già un segreto:
Che partivo già pensando a tornare indietro.
Anche se avevo altri parenti in alt'Italia
In Svizzera, nel Canada, in Argentina, Australia
Sangue del mio sangue che è sparso sull'atlante,
Ancora oggi odio chi disprezza l'emigrante
E ripensandoci poteva andarmi peggio
Ma mamma ha vinto il concorso e si torna a Reggio
Come la pioggia riporta alla fonte il fiume
La casa è dove è il cuore e non è un luogo comune.

Rit: Ho gli occhi all'orizzonte fin da quando ero bambino
Mio padre mi diceva parole che non capivo
Lo capisco adesso perché adesso il mio destino
Sono io che lo scrivo, sono io che lo scrivo.

Ho gli occhi all'orizzonte fin da quando ero bambino
Mio padre mi diceva parole che non capivo
Lo capisco adesso perché adesso ciò che vivo

Mi dà un nuovo motivo per ogni nuovo respiro

Crescendo raggiungevo qualche piccola vittoria
A scuola ero il migliore in italiano e storia
Le prime borse di studio messe alla posta
A centomila a centomila che il futuro costa.
E dopo era la vita di un ragazzo calabrese
Di botte non ne ho date più di quante ne abbia prese
A quindici anni gridavo "la vita è mia",
Scontri in piazza, fasci, manganelli e polizia
E ho visto sangue per terra e pistole a scuola
Amici del pallone uccisi per mezza parola.
E ho visto gente cambiare cognome e accento
Ma il posto da cui provengono resta dentro
Ed i mafiosi sui muri della città
Non dicono DC ma Casa delle Libertà
'95, qua la storia non migliora
Ho diciotto anni, faccio le valigie e parto ancora.

E mi ritrovo a Roma io ragazzo di provincia
Tra l'università e un millennio che comincia
Intanto mille palchi, mille fatti, mille scazzi
E continuavo a cercare il mare in mezzo ai palazzi.
Lavoro da precario ben oltre l'orario
Scrivevo ma le rime non pagavano il salario
E adesso sono grande, ho un mutuo sulle spalle
E nessun capitale se non cervello e palle.
Guardo lo specchio, a novembre sono trentuno
E non ho mai fatto una striscia né sparato a nessuno
Ho varie cicatrici, ricordi infelici
Ma un sole ben più forte nelle radici.
E non sono dalla parte dei vincenti
Ma conosco il mio futuro ed i suoi occhi verdi
Ed ho molte più favole che lacrime da scrivere
Se lei mi sorride non mi resta che viverle.

**"Musica Rivoluzione" (from the album by Kento & The
  Voodoo Brothers "Radici")**

Il suono è caldo come il sole ma ha il colore della notte
Ha un cuore uguale al nostro però batte più forte
Rughe sul viso, ed ha il sorriso di un bastardo
Guarda la morte in faccia e la morte abbassa lo sguardo
Io le so bene le risposte che sa darmi
E grido solo per la via come Giovanni da più di trent'anni

Per questo parlo: per la gente senza fiato
Per chi non ha tempo e sogna un tempo indeterminato
In testa musica, ma niente tra le mani
In cuffia al capolinea a Piazzale dei Partigiani
Scrivo per Reggio e per chi vive alla giornata
Scrivo un'altra Avvelenata sopra i muri della strada
Scrivo una nota e una parola, io ci credo ancora
Scrivo "Cuba Libre" e non intendo rum e cola
E l'ho già detto che di fatto siamo in tanti
Questa è musica, rivoluzione dentro i vostri impianti

Io scrivo rime e lascio fogli sul mio tavolo
Non dormono e mi parlano con la voce del diavolo
Mi sveglio e ogni testo lo trovo diverso
Più sarcastico e col plastico che cola da ogni verso
Sangue nuovo nelle arterie di questo quartiere
Suono forte, suono vero, ma non suono bene
Giro con gente che la pensa come me
E la musica ci salva, Rock The Casbah come i Clash.
È meglio un cerchio intorno al fuoco che un palco lontano
È meglio perdere la voce che parlare piano
Per questo è raro che scriva testi al passato:
Perché ogni giorno è struggle, come il pezzo dei Kalafro
E in vecchi dischi i musicisti sanno cosa sia
E perché il chitarrista vende l'anima ad un crocevia
E in vecchi dischi i musicisti l'hanno detto
Che la musica è la rivoluzione nello specchio.


**"Ciò che non siamo" (from the album "Sacco o Vanzetti")**
Quest'è l'ultimo passo, terzo atto dell'opera
parto verso Chtulhu a braccetto con Lovecraft

e nella mente commedie e grotteschi drammi
di poeti infelici morti giovani a 30 anni
liquido crepuscolo, saga del minuscolo
anche il cuore è un muscolo, non so più se è giusto o no
e la mia donna scompare tra i paraventi, palpebre assenti
mi svuota i sentimenti, versa paraffina sopra i cinque sensi
e più mi riempie la testa più io riempio quaderni.
Parlo plurale perché a nome di una generazione
Ma cerco da solo la soluzione.
Compassi (con passi) su noi stessi, troppi giri di parecchi
Ma vedo che purtroppo non c'è un Giotto che mi cerchi
Muse inquietanti ad ogni angolo
E chiedo al foglio "perché non parli?" come Michelangelo.

Rit: Sappiamo cò che non siamo, ciò che non vogliamo
restiamo dei poeti che non parlano italiano,
è un vento freddo ma ci porterà lontano
verso il brusco finale del crepuscolo umano.

E se il sogno regge il mondo come il titano Atlante
Sarò allo stesso tempo Don Chisciotte e Cervantes
Orlando e cantastorie, attore e Rossellini,
Piero e De Andrè, macchinista e Guccini.
Ho i segni di millenni di sconfitte sul mio volto
Porto la bandiera della parte del torto.
Perfino per chi mi ama io sarò morto
Come un Cristo mai risorto dal suo sepolcro.
Un Adamo che non ha la coscienza dell'io
Se l'indice di Dio non ha toccato il mio
Un tagadà che gira, ma la giostra si è fermata
La vita è una drammatica ironica sciarada.
Rinomino il domino, tessere con lettere
In parte si fanno arte se le sai mettere
E andremo lontani senza lasciare tracce
Siamo dadi, ma con uno su tutte le facce.

Non sono un gangsta rapper, non sono un conscious rapper
Sono, in quanto cogito, allergico alle etichette
Lirico nichilismo le cifre mi stanno strette

Sono il doppio zero in mezzo al 2007.
La follia di Nietzsche mi conduce
Come Carlos Castaneda apro porte, cerco luce.
Ma resta l'ombra la compagna del mio viaggio
Disegnerò sante puttane come in Caravaggio
Simboleggia quel buio verso cui tendo
orologi molli, la precarietà del tempo.
Perdonale signore le fanciulle in fiore,
mi riportano dieci anni indietro con un solo nome.
Fuori dai limiti, l'identikit è un limerick
chiamatemi Ismaele come l'incipit di Moby Dick
Bestemmie del papa, un'arte improvvisata
My way come Sinatra, parole a caso, dada.

**"Sacco o Vanzetti" (from the album "Sacco o Vanzetti")**
Voce come luce, ma se non c'è più calore
L'urlo blocca le parole, causa eclissi di sole.
Sacco Nicola, provenienza il meridione
Destinazione morte e nel frattempo la prigione.
Dentro quattro mura anche i pensieri chiusi a chiave.
Da 'sta serratura neanche l'aria può passare
Quando ho paura chiudo gli occhi e vedo il mare,
Sogno il cielo la mia terra e la mia donna da baciare.
Sogno ali di farfalle per passare tra le sbarre,
Mani di titani per piegarle.
Vorrei la forza per un nuovo capitolo,
Se ognuno dei miei passi non portasse al patibolo.
Anarchico e straniero, non assassino,
Lo sa perfino il giudice che ha scritto il mio destino.
Ed io ho scritto sopra il muro, a lettere nere:
"La giustizia non fa parte di un sistema di potere".

Vanzetti:
Voce come bomba, se la verità che abbiamo
Spezza il braccio teso nel saluto romano.
Vanzetti Bart, sono colpevole
Di odiare l'ingiustizia del sistema e le sue regole.
Di essere italiano, anarchico, emigrante,

Sindacalista, antifascista, militante
E la mia gente non si scorda più il passato
Con me presenta il conto di ogni secondo sprecato
A lavorare in nero come schiavi del padrone,
In file senza fine negli uffici immigrazione.
Signor giudice, è tutta una montatura!
L'ho vista quella penna che tremava di paura.
Scriveva una condanna che è la nostra vittoria,
Scriveva i nostri nomi sui libri di storia,
E tutti quanti ora lo devono sapere:
"La giustizia non fa parte di un sistema di potere".


## "No al Ponte" (from the album by Kalafro "Resistenza Sonora")

È uno spot elettorale in vista delle regionali
Un regalo di Natale per mafiosi e criminali
Mi ha detto un architetto che è sbagliato anche il progetto
Cantieri come squarci nel cuore dello Stretto
Certa gente non capisce che sarà un'Apocalisse
Altri contano i profitti sull'asse delle ascisse
Se tornasse Ulisse in questo mare che farebbe?
Prenderebbe i suoi guerrieri e come ieri lotterebbe!
Se tornasse Franco Nisticò cosa direbbe?
"Uniti per la lotta e il bene della nostra gente!"
Voglio risposte concrete senza retorica
Da Giampilieri alla 106 Jonica
Chi c'ha una voce e una coscienza deve dirlo:
È solo un monumento al Presidente del Consiglio
E intorno a noi ci sta un milione di persone
Che dice "No al ponte" come questa canzone.


## "Un giorno mi hai chiesto di spiegarti cos'è" (from the album "Sacco o Vanzetti")

È il posto dove il sangue scorre caldo e calmo
E riposo gambe stanche dopo un anno camminando
È il momento di silenzio tra parole di canzoni
È come mille cose, ma è senza paragoni.

È pura matematica, preciso come l'algebra
Ma in mezzo batte forte come i tamburi in Africa.
È Zion per i Rasta, Francesco per mia madre,
Libertà per mio nonno dopo un anno dentro un Lager.
È la conferma che un istante è importante,
Ma alla cassa seguirà il rullante, il sasso si farà diamante.
Poche parole, lenzuola stese al sole
Così bianche che sembravano brillare di quel non colore.
E le fissavo così tanto da bambino
Che se poi chiudevo gli occhi mi restava il negativo.
Sono le ultime sillabe in ogni rima
Ed il primo disegno sul mio quaderno in prima.

È dentro il tuo sorriso, sul tuo vestito nuovo
È casa e ogni mattone vale ore di lavoro
Era Montale quando scrisse dei limoni,
Miles Davis che toglieva note dagli assoli.
Semplice e puro, più buono che bello
È fede, ma di certo non si ferma a quell'anello.
E nasce piccolo che può dormirti in tasca,
Fallo rosso e che stia in alto come le bandiere in piazza.
È questo ed altro che non so dire
È un cerchio come un vinile, ha vite per puntine.
E non rimane moltro altro da capire...
Vuoi fermarlo? Ferma il sole la mattina in mezzo al suo salire.
E quel percorso vale più di ogni suo metro
Proprio come la parola vale più dell'alfabeto
Proprio come la musica è più che beat e rap
Proprio come "noi" siamo più che io e te.

**"Avrà i tuoi occhi" (from the album "Sacco o Vanzetti")**
Scrivo cifre con matite mentre conto banconote
Settembre giù al sud, notte blu come le note
Nel locale ho ballerine, bari, bluesmen e jazzisti
E servo tazze da tè colme all'orlo di buon whisky
Tequila e marijuana da Tijuana, cognac dalla Francia, Cohiba
    dall'Havana
Odio i federali ma gli sbirri locali

Qua montano di guardia come al circolo ufficiali
Per cui le banconote non sono mai poche
Sorrido come il diavolo al mio tavolo da poker
Che pure se mollassi non c'è da lamentarsi
Quattro milioni in banca come in mano quattro assi
Arrivato clandestino nella stiva di un veliero
Dieci anni e mille drammi dopo in mano c'ho un impero
E non metterti contro, l'italiano fa sul serio
Questo paese è mio non chiamarmi più straniero.

Si fa silenzio nel locale, solo vederla entrare
Mi colpisce come un gancio al plesso solare .
Vestito in seta bianca ed occhi di smeraldo
Non parlo ma ricambio ogni suo sguardo caldo
Nessuno la conosce o immagina chi sia
Tra tutti questi uomini nessuno dice "è mia"
E resta senza fiato il capo della polizia
Perché dentro quegli occhi vede fuoco ed anarchia.
Ma tutto 'sto silenzio mi dà ai nervi e non lo tollero
Qui comando io ed il solo dio è il dollaro!
Mi toccherà spiegarlo a tutta questa gente
Chi ha ragione qui, non è sempre il cliente
E mi avvicino verso quella sconosciuta
Sorrido "prego miss, si metta seduta"
Faccio segno al bancone: due bicchieri del migliore
E poi gioco la mia mano come quando fuori piove.

E nel locale non c'è un suono né una nota
Ogni candela è spenta, ogni bottiglia è vuota
Le ragnatele sopra i muri come affreschi
Guardo negli occhi persone e vedo teschi
Tutto il mio presente sembra così distante
Soltanto lei rimane bella ed elegante
Sorride e resta muta, è sempre lì seduta
Ma adesso lo sa bene che l'ho riconosciuta
Mille volte mi è passata accanto mentre guidavo stanco
O quando rilanciavo contro il banco
Mille volte mi ha preso e lasciato andare
Come chi partiva promettendo di tornare

Ed altre mille volte l'ho chiamata e non veniva
Ed io sputavo bile nel soffrire alla deriva
Ma ora lei è qui le dico "ok, ci siamo,
"Non dirmi dove andiamo ma tienimi per mano".

Leggimi il futuro nei tarocchi
O sui fondi di bicchieri rotti
Verrà la morte e avrà i tuoi occhi
E non so dove né quando
Ma so che sto aspettando
La morte col tuo stesso sguardo

**"Dear Brother" (from the album by Kento & The Voodoo Brothers "Radici")**
Non credo in questo stato, oggi come ieri
Alle lapidi incise e alle divise dei carabinieri
La violenza è solo loro, noi non siamo uguali
Vecchie città, nuove retate nei centri sociali
E il vostro oro il nostro sangue non lo può comprare
Morti sul lavoro, stessi fiori rossi sulle bare
Suona a Rosarno ed in Sicilia, suona in tutto il Sud
In Val di Susa e nell'acciaio della ThyssenKrupp
Io quando scrivo l'inchiostro buca la pagina
Il futuro è la poesia, la fantasia di chi lo immagina
dopo 20 anni stessa lotta e stesso palco
pugni alti e kefiah in faccia come nel '94
E chi non urla o non ha voce oppure non ha fede
ma il capitale è sempre uguale:  è sempre in malafede
Io faccio musica e so che il domani
sta nei segni sulla faccia, sopra i calli delle mani.

**"Struggle" (from the album by Kalafro "Resistenza Sonora")**
Guardati intorno e scoprirai perché combatto
ho piani di battaglia sul mio rhymebook, tecniche d'assalto
scarpe sull'asfalto e gli occhi al blu cobalto
devo sognare il doppio perché in troppi non sognano affatto

Reggio Calabria city e dite di capirci
ma il rispetto costa caro e un proiettile due spicci
Ecco perché ogni rima è calda come il Sahara
e il suono ferma in aria il colpo dell'infame quando spara
Colpisco forte senza usare la lupara
se ci stai dietro senti l'eco espandersi in tutta l'Italia
Alzo il volume finché il basso abbatte le pareti
Kento dà una voce alla rivolta del 2010.

Ed ogni nota risuona come una bomba
Ogni rima taglia un comma della norma perché
    controinforma
Con questo testo spezzo il ponte sullo Stretto
brucio i soldi della mafia per le firme sul progetto
Se gli uomini d'onore sono i primi tra gli infami
che hanno il sangue degli onesti sulle mani, qui non c'è
    domani
Tengo distinti il giornalismo e la notizia
Tengo distinti il giudice, il giudizio e la giustizia...
E quello che ci hanno rubato non ritorna
nonostante tutti i ceri alla Madonna che ha acceso mia nonna
I soldi fanno i soldi, la fame fa la fame
Se muoio porta un fiore per fumare e versa vino in mare
Se sopravvivo un altro giorno per lottare
ogni parola sarà rivoluzione per chi sa ascoltare
Quello che senti se spegni il telegiornale
è Babylon che crolla sotto il peso del suo stesso male.


"Resistenza Sonora" (from the album by Kalafro
    "Resistenza Sonora")
È Resistenza Sonora in strada e sulla scena,
scrivo e controinformo contro il cloroformio del sistema.
Si combatte, il suono butta giù le maschere
e tre quarti del music market non ha carattere.
Nuovi guerriglieri, briganti come ieri,
non voglio boss, ma nemmeno sbirri e giustizieri:
battaglie in strada come a Santa Clara
e una maglietta di Guevara vale solo quanto l'hai sudata.

Passaparola come si passa la giolla,
dai una lezione di storia ai "boia chi molla";
partono ancora i treni per Reggio Calabria
ed ogni strage che s'insabbia fa più aspra la nostra rabbia.
Dedicato alle radici dentro,
a chi sta al nord da trent'anni e non ha perso l'accento:
rivoluzione in ogni mia parola
e nella gente che la suona... Resistenza Sonora.

**"Stalingrado" (from the album "Sacco o Vanzetti")**
Tensione che ci uccide, e non mi dire di sorridere
Chiedimi di lottare, perché lottare è vivere.
Non credo alle sirene del successo
Io non sono il prossimo nessuno sono il primo me stesso.
E se la vittima è la musica e l'accusa è di omicidio
Io uccido le stelle della radio come il video.
Dipingo con i testi perché il rap che porto avanti
Sporca in rosso tonache nere e colletti bianchi.
E non mi fotte se c'hai la pistola, polvere nella stagnola
gli MC che nomini su' omini senza pisciola
Rivoluzione in ogni mia parola
E in chi la spinge da Milano a Palermo, e non è Raul Bova.
Continua evoluzione come un writer con il lettering
Spingo chi c'ha i concetti, non chi dice di averceli.
E se questa è una guerra chi decide il risultato?
La musica, l'ultima trincea di Stalingrado.

Rit: Per chi sa che è una guerra e che è uno scontro quotidiano
Per chi resisterà con ogni mezzo necessario
Per chi resta fuori dalla moda e dallo stadio
La musica è l'ultima trincea di Stalingrado.

E siamo in tanti, e non ancora disillusi
Io guardo avanti, nel cielo coi diamanti come Lucy
Segnali sound ribelli ti sputtanano il Blackberry
Canto amore col dolore nel cuore come Otis Redding
Sangue sul mio rhymebook, conta un milione di pagine
E non cambio una parola perché me l'ha detto un manager

L'etichetta fashion non apprezza il mio progetto
Le mie rime non le pagano, quindi non hanno prezzo.
Un rapper sa che è meglio un lavoro precario
Che dare il culo per un contratto e i passaggi in radio
E un rapper sa che andrà sempre a finire male
Se l'industria della musica è serva del capitale.
Senza nazione né bandiera se è di quest'Italia,
Siamo guerrieri nella notte e non c'è Coney Island.
Resta resistere con ogni mezzo necessario
Musica, ultima trincea di Stalingrado.

Rit: La musica è un filo teso, è il filo del microfono
È fuoco, gioco, sfogo, pogo, è il logos del filosofo.
E ciò che la classifica massifica
Quello che copre le bugie del Vaticano coi Magnificat.
La musica mi ha chiesto cento e dato mille in cambio
Perché sta muto chi è venduto, non solo chi è stanco
Mille canzoni e stacchetti sui palinsesti
E sette note come fiori sulle tombe di Sacco e Vanzetti.
La vera musica va oltre le parole
È come l'alta tensione, a volte chi la tocca muore.
Va oltre lo strumento, il tempo, il sample
È terribilmente serio chi la suona sorridendo
È un supremo amore come John Coltrane
Non si fida dei Re Mida né dei beat da hit parade.
Io resto fuori dalla moda e dallo stadio
La musica è l'ultima trincea di Stalingrado.

**"Roots Music" (from the album by Kento & The Voodoo
    Brothers "Radici")**
La radice del mio suono sta nel canto popolare
Storia scritta con il sangue sulle lame delle spade
Roots music, la cantano gli esclusi
Col segno meno in banca e in tasca solo i pugni chiusi
E gli invasori ci hanno imposto i loro santi
Col nostro pane in bocca ci hanno chiamato briganti
Il sud del mondo ha più blues di Robert Johnson
Ed il futuro è nostro solamente se ricordo

Perché dalla rabbia nasce la nuova coscienza
E qui vecchie macerie sono nuove fondamenta
Parlo in dialetto con rispetto ai nostri anziani
viviamo anni lontani, ma so che siamo uguali
So che siamo pietra della Magna Grecia
Siamo carta del poeta contro la carta moneta
E non è nostalgia delle radici
Si chiama vita, appartenenza, sangue, amore, cicatrici.

Canto la saga invisibile di ogni figlio di Annibale
E l'amaro nelle rime è l'antico male di vivere
Siamo gli sconfitti, i migranti, i bastardi
Lo stato uccide ma a noi dice "state calmi"
Se fosse vero basterebbe solo il sole
Però quella canzone dice "brigante se more"
Se ci fosse un dio avrebbe gli occhi di mio nonno
Ma non avrebbe il cuore di riviverne ogni giorno
Il colonialismo cambia faccia, non sostanza
Oggi ha la stessa arma e i soldi di ogni banca
Io ho i libri dei filosofi, il volume dei microfoni
E nel mio accento le voci di cento popoli
Ho sempre scelto e sempre la parte sbagliata
E il disco non è bello ma pesa una tonnellata
Un altro giorno con la lotta e la memoria
Un'altra spinta dal basso sulla ruota della storia.


### H.I.P. H.O.P. (HO IDEE POTENTI, HO OBIETTIVI PRECISI) – (from the album by Kento & The Voodoo Brothers "Da Sud")

Oggi non è più il momento di essere indecisi
Ho idee potenti, ho obiettivi precisi
Finché è il capitale a generare le sue crisi
Ho idee potenti, ho obiettivi precisi

Per chi giudica l'arte dai contratti e dagli ascolti
L'Hip-Hop è vivissimo, siete voialtri i morti
In strada c'è un fermento di cui non volete accorgervi
Cultura e resistenza tra cariche e lacrimogeni

La nostra libertà è necessità sulla mia pagina
Antifa, sul muro è enorme la scritta Partizan
Chi controlla il panico tiene il ferro dal manico
Qua scrivere è lottare da intellettuale organico
Nei campi profughi b-boy sopra il cemento
Smash the Wall, Reggio-Palestina, crew che rappresento
Da Rosarno alla Valsusa il movimento cosa ascolta?
Porto amore e rap dal vivo in ogni luogo della lotta
Troppi mc da discoteca, troppi gangsta da tastiera
Ciò che conta per davvero è ciò che sta sotto il New Era
Non si compra questo amore, le bestemmie ed i sorrisi
Ho idee potenti, ho obiettivi precisi.

Questa scena è solo scena per fare i buffoni in rete
Nei quartieri gangsta veri fanno quello che scrivete
Mc bagna il microfono nel fuoco di una molotov
E un rapper sarà in grado di dare una voce a un popolo
Non dirmi "sono bravi" se hanno liriche da idioti:
l'hardcore è questo testo oppure dirci quanto scopi?
Il mercato sponsorizza il rapper che lo pubblicizza
Ma se manca la sostanza fumerai solo la Rizla
Questo è dedicato a chi a volte pensa di smettere
Combatti ciò che siamo per ciò che potremmo essere
Se c'era chi diceva che il cielo è l'unico limite
L'oro è nel sottosuolo, non in cima alle classifiche
E spero che un domani, riascoltando i nostri dischi
Non diremo che avevamo i mezzi e non li abbiamo visti
Non saremo più pedine, non più solo né divisi
Con idee potenti e obiettivi precisi.

**"Briganti" (from the album by Kalafro "Resistenza Sonora")**
Parola vera, la posta è alta come i De La,
lirica Guernica, Apocalisse la mia tela,
che fiducia, oggi che nessuno è più al sicuro,
carta brucia, Fahrenheit 451.
Reggio Calabria dov'è quasi sempre estate,
dove volano molti proiettili e poche minchiate.

La gioventù che resta pensa solo a sé
e nella merda fuma più erba di Dr. Dre,
eh sì che urla, perché nessuno sta a sentire
e spinge forte perchè è affamata da morire.
I nostri sguardi sono i soli che non cambiano,
ascolto Bob canta "War inna Babylon".
Combattiamo come abbiamo sempre fatto,
pugni alti e kefiah in faccia come nel '94,
fogli coi pensieri, sogni e desideri,
scusate ma non canto il vostro Inno di Mameli.

Se l'ansia del futuro è un sole scuro su 'sta Terra,
l'oggi brucia l'atmosfera tipo effetto serra
per la mia gente non c'è trucco e non c'è maschera,
nessun Barack Obama a dirgli che possono farcela.
La città che sorride coi giornalisti
dopo dice Crucifige a troppi poveri Cristi
ed il presente a volte genera i suoi drammi,
a volte dà in mano un microfono a un ragazzo a 15 anni.
Ogni giorno sopra il Corso celebra i suoi dei,
ogni notte canta il blues come Lady Day
e non c'è stadio, non c'è droga, non c'è via d'uscita,
la vita scorre come sangue da questa ferita.
Mille colori insieme fanno un solo grigio,
passa un pezzo in radio dice Losing My Religion,
spengo la radio, mi gioco quel che ho,
chiudo un'altra strofa, chant down Babylon.


**Inno Rugby Team No Tav – No Ponte – No Muos (2013)**
Da Niscemi alla Clarea tu scendi in campo che ti aspetto
Qua la spinta della mischia spezza il ponte sullo Stretto
vecchi pazzi e lottatori, difendiamo i territori
dall'attacco di mafiosi, marines e speculatori
la mia banda non ha un soldo, ha testa e cuore che funziona
tengo il tempo, e al terzo tempo bevo con gli All Reds a Roma
solo mare nello Stretto, solo verde in Val di Susa
e in Sicilia cieli aperti, non colonialismo USA
tu supporta questa squadra e se solo la lotta paga

voce in alto e mani in aria quando parte un'altra haka
paradenti e respingenti contro corpi contundenti:
Robocop, Rambo in divisa sono servi dei potenti
coi ragazzi e le ragazze, con il sole e il temporale,
con il tifo che si alza e rimbalza la palla ovale
vecchie glorie di quartiere e giovanotti sui vent'anni
spingi forte, passa indietro, corri sempre verso avanti.

## Hip-Hop Smash the Wall (2014)

Più forte di una bomba, più a fondo di una tomba
La musica sostiene questa terra e la circonda
Poche chiacchiere, ho il suono per combattere
Sto davanti al muro e la mia voce lo può abbattere
L'urlo sale forte a Reggio come qui a Ramallah,
ma se devo aver paura temo solo chi non parla
odio il pregiudizio e l'ignoranza del razzista
"Meridionale? Mafia", "Palestina? Terrorista"
Israele uccide ma il proiettile è italiano
Democrazia diretta, sì, diretta dal denaro
Per questo quando suono non sentitevi al sicuro
La lotta va veloce, la mia voce abbatte il muro.

## IL DEBITO (2016)

Tutte le generazioni della mia famiglia sono partite.
L'Australia, gli Stati Uniti, la Svizzera, il Nord
—"l'Altitalia", come si diceva ancora quand'ero piccolo.

E tutte le generazioni della mia famiglia sono tornate, e io per
        ultimo
sono cresciuto con il mare e il sole,
come sono cresciute
tutte le generazioni della mia famiglia,
prima di partire.

A diciott'anni sono partito anch'io,
come mio padre, e mio nonno, e i loro padri e nonni prima di
        loro.

Io, io però non so se tornerò,
e onestamente il blues della lontananza
non lo capisce solo chi non l'ha mai provato.

A volte, per una settimana intera sogno di essere a casa.
Letteralmente: per sette notti consecutive chiudo gli occhi
e c'è mia nonna che prepara le polpette,
e c'è il fresco della veranda
e l'aria di festa in casa
di ogni volta che tornavo e torno.

Potremmo essere ricchi, lo penso davvero.
Potremmo fare che l'orgoglio,
non sia un salvadanaio di latta
con gli stessi pochi spicci di rame
che scuotendo lo fanno suonare
e a noi ci pare di essere contenti.

Potremmo ridere dell'onore finto
degli uomini d'onore finti
come se fosse il naso rosso dei pagliacci,
come se fosse una trombetta di plastica.

Potremmo fare nostra la terra nostra
e i soldi nostri, e le strade, e perfino gli uffici e il municipio
e il fatalismo – anche quando fa caldo –potrebbe non essere
più un muro o una pietra.

Potremmo non essere più colonia,
non più periferia,
potremmo sconfiggere il blues
di chi sta male qui, e peggio quando se ne va.

Potremmo essere giovani e migliori.
Potremmo forse, per una volta,
pagare il debito
di tutte le generazioni
che sono partite.

**"Il Blues del Bar" (from the album by Kento & The Voodoo Brothers "Radici")**
Nelle notti in cui non dormi parla il blues dei tuoi ricordi
Mille birre sono strane ninnananne per gli insonni
Stesso bar in quelle sere, con gli stessi quattro a bere
Scrivo grandi verità sul fondo di un sottobicchiere
Qualche anno prima stavo sulla stessa panca
Ma ero ancora più vicino ai vent'anni che ai 40
Però più scrivo in rima più mi accorgo che non cambi
Che sono uguale a prima tranne i debiti e i capelli bianchi
Ho questa traccia che mi abbraccia e mi circonda
E lei è sempre più bella perché si è fatta più donna
Mi faccio un sorso e il successivo, si parla del Che
Dei film di Volonté, di un mondo che qui non c'è
In mezzo a slot e videopoker, per chi non ha abbandonato
Il sogno a buon mercato del sottoproletariato
E ho capito che ogni notte c'è chi parla
Non per raccontare storie ma per non scordarle all'alba

Quaggiù un'altra notte calda come il Sud
Tu paga un altro giro di quel rum
Il suono riempie queste sere quindi mettiti a sedere
E versati un altro bicchiere.

Siamo tristi ed umani come i bar delle stazioni
E i binari sono pensieri, e i passeggeri note di canzoni
Sogni passati nei ricordi delle estati
Se la vita serve amari, caffè al vetro e distillati
E il vestito più diverso molto spesso è un diversivo
Però il buio è comprensivo quindi ognuno è un antidivo
Stanotte al bar racconta troppe verità
Tra chi canta per amore e chi bestemmia per necessità
Sbirri in borghese per reprimere l'illecito
Ma l'erba in questa guerra ha più soldati dell'esercito
Throw-up nero e argento, cemento, vandali ed arte
Liti per dieci carte, ritmi in levare e battere

Densa come nafta, breve solo sulla carta
Tra i fantasmi come Kafka ma non so mai dirle basta
La notte è donna è in quanto tale devi amarla
Le racconti le tue storie e lei se ne scorda all'alba


**"Voodoo" (from the album by Kento & The Voodoo
Brothers "Radici")**
Stanotte il suono è voodoo e cola sangue già dal check
Kento microphone guerriglia, gorilla silverback
rivoluzionario vengo su dalla provincia
Mordo alla giugulare, altri si mordono la lingua
Moltiplico la voce, quando rimo è come un coro
E non ho fatto un nuovo disco, ho fatto un disco nuovo
Mai un pupazzo nelle mani dello Stato
Ed il mio eroe non è un prete né un magistrato
Io sto col Sud e la sua gente ed i suoi guai
E ogni rima che ti lancio è come un gancio di Lenny Bottai
Nel mio curriculum lo studio del reale
1000 libri, 1000 dischi e tipo centomila strade
suonano Kento nella manifestazione
mentre troppi dischi d'oro sono plastica e cartone
Io sputo a terra e rido di 'sta babilonia

Suono più crudo, il loro voodoo con me non funziona.
Stanotte suona Voodoo, spingo il suono più scuro
Spilli dentro agli occhi, nessuno è più al sicuro
Stanotte suona Voodoo, spingo il suono più scuro
Il sistema che ci vuole faccia al muro colpirà più duro

Se il ricco tratta il mondo come fosse solo suo
Io tifo Val di Susa, no ponte, no MUOS.
Kento, Voodoo brothers, Ice One, che vuoi dirci?
Bevo insieme ad Havoc, suono RC to Queensbridge.
Questo è Voodoo come il blues in Louisiana
Scorro come il Mississippi tra i conflitti di 'sta vita amara
E se l'Hip-Hop oggi è morbido è pulito
sono sporco, legno vecchio, metallo arrugginito
Sangue di pollo sui feticci di 'sta società

con sempre più reality e sempre meno realtà
Questo è il proiettile della rivoluzione
Colto nel momento esatto in cui colpisce il dittatore
Per cui non sono in fila nei locali fashion
Ma a bere birra dietro al palco del concerto
Porto rivolta sulla strada e sulla scena
Ogni mente indipendente spezza il voodoo del sistema.

**"Hazet 36" (from the album by Kento & The Voodoo
Brothers "Radici")**
Io cerco ancora una parola per cantarla
tra pagine di libri o in equilibro sul mio pentagramma
voglio che il sangue scorra in mezzo alle sue lettere
mosaico senza tessere, un semplice trasmettere
che non faccia miracoli, ma porti luce agli angoli
come certi dischi di Guccini e di Pietrangeli
cantastorie più che cantautore
ma, se è unica la musica, passami il testimone
frasi su quaderni ancora incendiano le menti
costruiscono universi con la voce e gli strumenti
la repressione dura dai tempi di Valle Giulia
ma la mia gente non scappa, è più forte della paura
e il nostro inchiostro nero si fa polvere da sparo
non resta che resistere, è una nuova Stalingrado
e se il nemico resta quello di quegli anni
lo abbiamo già sconfitto e oggi abbiamo nuove armi.

Io so che senza musica domani sarà peggio
Il silenzio ghiaccia l'aria pure a ferragosto a Reggio
Il piombo dei '70 oggi è la polvere bianca
Chi è schiavo giù a Rosarno e chi è schiavo di una banca
alza il volume della cassa o la chitarra
non arriverà alla massa se chi canta non ne parla
antagonista ad ogni finta alternativa
il mio microfono è la Hazet 36 degli anni 2000
per questo metto le parole in uno stereo
e ho il tormento di un poeta ma senza averne il genio
suono più forte di plastico e Kalashnikov

mi ascoltano i ragazzi in piazza e qualche vecchio anarchico
anti-stato ma ho memoria del passato
e so che la libertà non sta nel libero mercato
e parlo chiaro perché è chiaro ciò che ho dentro
resto sempre in movimento, la rivoluzione è vento.

**"Vengo da Sud" (from the album by Kento & The Voodoo
   Brothers "Da Sud")**
Il cuore di chi lotta è una bestia selvatica
Sta stretto prigioniero nella gabbia toracica
Un pugno chiuso contro il cielo, in faccia una lacrima
Vengo da Sud, ti dico: vengo da Sud

Non è un ritorno, io non sono mai andato via
La stessa faccia, stesse lotte, stesse barricate
Lo stesso odio per fascisti e borghesia
Kento scorre ancora come il sangue nelle strade
Vengo da Sud come la mafia ed il dialetto
Senti l'accento in ogni sillaba che dico
Sono un figlio di briganti, un maledetto
Gesù mi ama, io lo vedo più come un amico
E finti gangsta fanno una finta guerra
In palio la classifica e due grammi di mannite
La mafia vera intanto uccide la mia terra
Voi rapper davvero non sapete ciò che dite
E l'ho già detto: la mia voce è come un coro
Io sono il Sud che oggi è sparso in tutta Italia
Per questo quando rimo non sono mai solo
Sul palco siamo centinaia di migliaia.

Ho scritto un verso per ognuno dei compagni morti
E so che l'aldilà probabilmente non esiste
Per cui per Valarioti e Nisticò, per tutti i nostri
La sola eternità la tiene in pugno chi resiste
La mente di chi lotta è una bestia selvatica
Piena d'amore tanto quanto sembra ostile
Stretta prigioniera nella scatola cranica
Solo chi sente che spinge lo può capire

E non pensavo che di noi meridionali
Oggi potesse dirsi che ci manca la memoria:
Ma come fai a dire "Italia agli italiani"
Se tuo padre ha subito il razzismo in prima persona?
Stanotte scrivo, il vino macchia la mia carta
Però va bene, pare che porti fortunaOgni città del resto è a
    Sud di un'altra
Tranne se vivi al polo Nord o sulla luna.

**"Totò Speranza" (from the album by Kento & The Voodoo**
    **Brothers "Da Sud")**
Il mio nome è Totò, e suono il basso in una band
28 anni, sogni grandi come i miei perché
intorno un mare azzurro finché l'occhio non si perde
e le onde sono come il loop ipnotico di un reggae
siamo gli Invece, un bel gruppo ed un bel nome
ci ascolta molta gente alle feste e all'occupazione
non sono un santo, ho fatto anch'io le mie cazzate
però un uomo senza errori non è un uomo, come fate?
marzo a Bovalino sembra già sia primavera
il vento soffia piano come piano si fa sera
ed una vita vera è meglio di una vita seria
e certa gente non è mai viva in una vita intera
ne giro una e poi l'accendo e poi sorrido
il fumo riempie l'aria ed è il mio ultimo respiro
si fa silenzio ed il buio riempie la stanza
stanotte racconta il sogno di Totò Speranza.

Da quassù vi guardo tutti e cazzo, siete sempre uguali
persi dietro stessi problemi e schemi mentali
dietro quel sistema che vi rende ancora schiavi
esseri umani, imparate ad essere umani
fratello mio ribellati, sorella mia combatti
amare questa terra nostra significa amarti
mentre invecchierete sarò giovane per sempre
Totò che guarda il mare con gli occhi di un ventottenne
con una canna accesa e l'aria di chi sfida il mondo
e se mi chiedi cosa voglio ti sorrido e non rispondo

guardati allo specchio, siamo la stessa persona
siamo entrambi dallo stesso lato di quella pistola
e la mia forza è l'amore che ci conquista
e la mia musica il tocco di ogni bassista
spezza il silenzio, ora il suono riempie la stanza
stanotte racconta il sogno di Totò Speranza.

## "Denise" (from the album by Kento & The Voodoo Brothers "Da Sud")

Denise mi guarda, sorride solo con gli occhi
dice che vede l'alba dopo troppi anni di notti
le luci stamattina sono come cocci rotti
lei gira calma, quasi trasparente in mezzo ai blocchi.
Intorno il traffico, ed è musica in delay
e specchi di pozzanghere che non sanno chi sei
intanto mi ripeto: il suo coraggio non l'avrei
ma provo a stare dritto con la schiena, come lei.
Pensa se perdessi tutto, come affronteresti il lutto
prendere il tuo cuore secco e farlo diventare un frutto.
Giornate amare, quando vorresti restare
ma l'amore non lo vuole chi non ha amore da dare.
Fosse per lei, Denise guarderebbe avanti
non vorrebbe più essere più vecchia dei suoi anni.
Non c'è più vento, forse il tempo oggi migliora...
fosse per lei, Denise amerebbe ancora.

Denise non crede che il mondo le giri intorno
cammina ancora e l'aurora spunta ogni giorno
certi barattano l'amore per l'orgoglio
come se loro stessi non ne avessero bisogno
ed a vent'anni tutti vogliono scappare
ma Denise è differente, tra la gente al funerale
nonostante le ferite sogna una vita normale
nell'abbraccio della piazza che le fa da cattedrale
per quanto io possa trovare le parole
se non hanno vita dentro non camminano da sole
e non è ciò che scrivi, ma quello che fai che parla
Denise non posso viverla, ma posso raccontarla.

Non trova spazio nei TG di mezza sera
la normalità assordante di una giovane guerriera
Denise non vuole che si dica che è un esempio
e in fondo pure questo è un passo verso il cambiamento.

Sorridi allora, sconfiggi la paura
Tu che sei il cambiamento camminerai sicura
La strada è dura e siamo nati senza ali
Ma la tua strada è l'unica che porterà a domani

**"Piazzale Loreto" (from the album by Kento & The Voodoo
    Brothers "Da Sud")**
Vedo i fascisti di ieri e di oggi, con giacca cravatta e la
    ventiquattrore
Portare il denaro che serve a pagare la mafia con la
    corruzione
Si chiama Mafia Capitale, è quel sistema elettorale
In cui il camerata serve perché fa il servo del capitale
E nei comizi fomentano l'odio, tengono il punto da bravo
    soldato
Odiano i rom, certo però non odiano i soldi che gli hanno
    portato
E una sinistra finta incassa e fa finta di niente
ma non dirti antifascista se fai business con sta gente
Porta i soldi, assegnano il bando, porta la celtica al collo
    Alemanno
Io porto fuoco e benzina in ogni mia rima e so che bruceranno
Solo odio per Casa Pound, Alba Dorata e i loro slogan
E per chi ha preso vecchia merda e l'ha chiamata Forza
    Nuova
Fino a ieri facevano i primi guardiani di muri puliti e decoro
Ora fanno convention di rap e graffiti per fare parlare di loro
Per questo porto resistenza, non un passo indietro
Ogni palco su cui salgo è piazzale Loreto

E dire che ormai non esiste il fascismo è la scusa
    dell'indifferente

Ha lavato la faccia, indossato la giacca e rimane la merda di
sempre
Io so che Dax resiste ancora ed odia chi lo uccide
Ogni giorno, col silenzio, in nome del suo quieto vivere
Io sto con gli stessi compagni di sempre che mi hanno
guardato la schiena
A scuola ed in piazza, il rap è una farsa, rifiuto sta merda di
scena
Com'è che certi discorsi li fa quasi solo Kento
Mentre voi non dite niente, come aveste il micro spento
Ne ho visti nei centri sociali spararsi le pose da mc militanti
Che bacerebbero il culo a Salvini se solo avessero i soldi
davanti
Noi siamo gli sconfitti che si prendono il domani
Siamo ricchi, sì, di tutto tranne i beni materiali
Finché ho una rima, sangue e saliva, penna sul foglio e sativa
Finché la lotta fa la differenza, la mia resistenza continua
Stasera questo posto è nostro, non si cede un metro
Ogni palco che calpesto è piazzale Loreto.

Rimango antifascista – piazzale Loreto
La fine del razzista è a piazzale Loreto
Per cambiare prospettiva deve stare a testa in giù
Non ti piace la mia musica? A lei non piaci tu.


**"La verità" (from the album "Sacco o Vanzetti")**
Non è nei governi né nei parlamenti, non siede al tavolo
insieme ai potenti
Non sta nei conti di nessuna banca, non l'hanno mai vista alla
Casa Bianca.
Nessun chirurgo le ha chiesto un consiglio mentre spianava le
rughe di Silvio
Non sta nei circoli di Forza Nuova né nei fascicoli di Lele
Mora.
Non sta nei "buongiorno" per abitudine di chi nasconde solo
solitudine
Non fa gli elogi a nessun funerale non sta nel non dire per
non fare male.

Non sta in silenzio né in troppi discorsi non è dovunque né in
   posti nascosti
Non è un gigante non è una farfalla non è dove dicono che
   puoi trovarla.

Rit: Non sta nei servizi dei telegiornali
Non sta in prima pagina sui quotidiani
Resta in silenzio in corsie d'ospedali
Urla fin troppo in  drammi familiari
Non sta nei servizi dei telegiornali
Non sta in prima pagina sui quotidiani
Sta con chi non legge sui palmi il domani
Sa essere un'arma per le stesse mani

La sento nei canti di rivoluzione, in ogni rivolta che affossa il
   padrone
La vedo sorridere incontro alla morte cantando che il vento
   ora fischia più forte
L'ho vista piangere Carlo Giuliani, sparare in montagna con i
   partigiani
L'ho vista splendere su volti ignoti e intrecciarsi ai capelli dei
   Rasta devoti
La chiesa di Roma l'ha dimenticata, l'ho vista un milione di
   volte ignorata.
A volte svela e a volte promette, e a volte sta in rima nei testi
   dei rappers
L'ho vista piangere nera di rabbia, negli occhi di disoccupati
   in Calabria
E sta nella storia, ma vive il presente, è il solo tesoro che è
   nostro per sempre.

# CROSSINGS

## AN INTERSECTION OF CULTURES

A refereed series, *Crossings* is dedicated to the publication of translations from Italian to English as well as texts in Italian. Open to all genres, translators and authors should first contact the editors before submitting a complete manuscript.

Rodolfo Di Biasio
*Wayfarers Four*
Trans. Justin Vitiello
Fiction. $11.00. Crossings 1

Isabella Morra
*Canzoniere: A Bilingual Edition*
Trans. Irene Musillo Mitchell.
Poetry. $9.00. Crossings 2

Nevio Spadone
*Lus*
Trans. Teresa Picarazzi
Theater. $7.00. Crossings 3

Flavia Pankiewicz
*American Eclipses*
Trans. P. Carravetta. Intro. J. Tusiani
Poetry. $9.00. Crossings 4

Dacia Maraini
*Stowaway on Board*
Trans. Gi. Bellesia &V. Offredi Poletto
Gender. $8.00. Crossings 5

Walter Valeri, ed.
*Franca Rame. Woman on Stage*
Theater. $18.00. Crossings 6

Carmine Biagio Iannace
*The Discovery of America:*
Trans. William Boelhower.
Autobiography. $15.00. Crossings 7

Romeo Musa da Calice
*Luna sul salice*
Trans. Adelia V. Williams
Folklore. $9.00. Crossings 8

Marco Paolini & Gabriele Vacis
*The Story of Vajont*
Trans. Thomas Simpson.
Theater. $13.00. Crossings 9

Silvio Ramat
*Sharing A Trip: Selected Poems*
Trans. Emanuel di Pasquale.
Poetry. $14.00. Crossings 10

Raffaello Baldini
*Carta canta (Page Proof)*
Ed. D. Benati. Trans. A. Bernardi.
Theater. $12.00. Crossings 11

Maura Del Serra
*Infinite Present: Selected Poems*
Trans. Emanuel Di Pasquale
& Michael Palma
Poetry. $14.00. Crossings 12

Dino Campana
*Canti Orfici*
Trans. & Notes Luigi Bonaffini
Poetry. $25.00. Crossings 13

Roberto Bertoldo
*The Calvary of the Cranes*
Trans. Emanuel di Pasquale.
Poetry. $15.00. Crossings 14

Paolo Ruffilli
*Like It or Not*
Trans. Ruth Feldmann
& James Laughlin
Poetry. $16.00. Crossings 15

Giuseppe Bonaviri
*Saracen Tales*
Trans. Barbara De Marco.
Fiction. $19.00. Crossings 16

Leonilde Frieri Ruberto
*Such Is Life*
Trans. Laura Riberto
Intro. Ilaria Serra
Autobiography. $10.00. Crossings 17

Gina Lagorio
*Tosca. The Cat Lady*
Trans. By Martha King
Thomas Simpson
Novel. $16.00. Crossings 18

Marco Martinelli
*Rumore di acque*
Translated and edited by
Thomas Simpson
Theater. $15.00. Crossings 19

Emanuele Pettener
*A Season in Florida*
Trans. Thomas De Angelis
Short Stories. $14.00. Crossings 20

Angelo Spina
*Il cucchiaio trafugato*
Novel. $16.00. Crossings 21

Michela Zanarella
*Meditations in the Feminine*
Trans. Leanne Hoppe
Poetry. $14.00. Crossings 22

www.ingramcontent.com/pod-product-compliance
Lightning Source LLC
LaVergne TN
LVHW041255080426
835510LV00009B/741